語学シリーズ
第❸巻

ボイス・オブ・アメリカ（VOA）
ニュースで学ぶ英語 レベル1

佐藤晶子 著

大学教育出版

はじめに

　ボイス・オブ・アメリカ（Voice of America: VOA）は米国政府運営の国営放送で，毎日ニュースを配信しています．本書では，パブリックドメイン *VOA Learning English: We are American English* で取り上げられたニュースを中心に，15 カテゴリーの記事に取り組み，終了時にはアメリカの概略を把握するとともに，TOEIC, TOEFL の出題形式に合わせた復習問題を解くことによって，実践的英語力の習得を目指します．

　読解のための語彙，文法および構文ノートは予習時の便宜を考え，ページの許す限り，できるだけ詳しくつけるようにしました．ただし，最初からノートに頼るのではなく，まず自分で辞書や参考書に当たることが大切です．

　ノートを付記するに際して，多くのリソースのお世話になりました．詳細を挙げることはできませんが，この場をお借りして感謝の意を表させていただきます．

　大阪大学杉田米行教授からは，本書を完成させるうえで貴重な助言をいただきました．代表取締役社長佐藤守氏と編集部安田愛氏には企画段階から大変お世話になりました．ここに心からお礼もうしあげます．

平成 26 年 9 月 1 日

著　者

本書の使い方

本書は自分で学習できるよう，次のような工夫を行っています．

① 記事のリスニング教材は *VOA Learning English*（http://learningenglish.voanews.com/）のサイトでダウンロードできます．URL を載せてありますので，そこにアクセスしてください．iPhone や Android スマートフォンでもアクセスできます．
② 記事をウェブサイト上で読みたい場合は，Google などの検索サイトで"voa"と課題文のタイトルを打ち込んで検索してください．例えば，「voa Losing Weight Proves」と打ち込むと，検索サイトでタイトルが出てきます．そのタイトルをクリックすると，課題文にアクセスすることができます．
③ スピーカーのマークをクリックすると英語の音声が流れます．
④ 本書のリーディング，リスニング課題の 内の数字は音声の経過時間です．予習復習の際に利用してください．Listening Comprehension は 30 秒以内，リーディングの課題箇所の時間は 5 分以内です．合計 6 分もあれば十分に聴き取れます．

VOA Learning English の教材は Level 1，Level 2 があります．Level 1 の英語は Level 2 よりもゆっくり流れます．本書はほとんどが Level 1 の教材で構成されています．Listening Comprehension は，動詞を聴き取ることに重点を置きました．English Composition も動詞を使いこなすことに重点を置いて出題しています．まず文章の先頭にある主語を聴き取り，次に内容を決定する肝心の動詞を聴き取ることができるよう練習してください．

本書では通常よりは遅めの英語を聴き取ることで，英語に慣れ，理解を深めることを目指します．ネイティヴの速度に近い英語を聴きたい人は，Level 2 や VOA（http://www.voanews.com/）のウェブサイトにアクセスしてください．記事英文と読み上げ音声の英語に不一致がある場合，必要であれば VOA ホームページに掲載された原文を参照してください．

ボイス・オブ・アメリカ（VOA）ニュースで学ぶ英語　レベル1

目　次

はじめに……………………………………………………………………………………… i
本書の使い方………………………………………………………………………………… ii

Unit1. Business
    Losing Weight Proves to Be Big Business ……………………………………… 1

Unit 2. Environment
    A Silent Killer – Carbon Monoxide Poisoning ………………………………… 6

Unit 3. Science and Technology
    Scientific and Engineering Inventions Save Lives …………………………… 11

Unit 4. History
    The American Civil War: Who Should Memorials Honor? ………………… 17

Unit 5. Agriculture
    Farmer Invents New Way to Grow Crops ……………………………………… 22

Unit 6. Finance
    For a New Nation, Hamilton Seeks a Bank …………………………………… 27

Unit 7. Government Politics
    President Adams Avoids War with France……………………………………… 32

Unit 8. Poverty
    U.S. Poverty Rate Highest Since 1993 ………………………………………… 38

Unit 9. Education
    Children at U.S. School Show Their Support for Victims in Japan ……… 43

Unit 10. Healthcare
    Have a headache? You are not alone …………………………………………… 48

Unit 11. Public Welfare
    People with Disabilities Achieve New Opportunities ················54

Unit 12. Law
    U.S. Supreme Court Upholds Health Care Law, Strikes Down
    Much of Immigration Law ················59

Unit 13. The Making of a Nation
    Christmas in 19th Century America ················65

Unit 14. Economy
    Americans Celebrate Thanksgiving by Eating, Serving
    and … Shopping? ················71

Unit 15. Ethnic
    New Study: Foreign Students Make U.S. Better, Faster ················76

訳例と解答················81
付録　役に立つサイト················103
参考文献················105

Unit 1 Business

Losing Weight Proves to Be Big Business

http://learningenglish.voanews.com/a/2263714.html

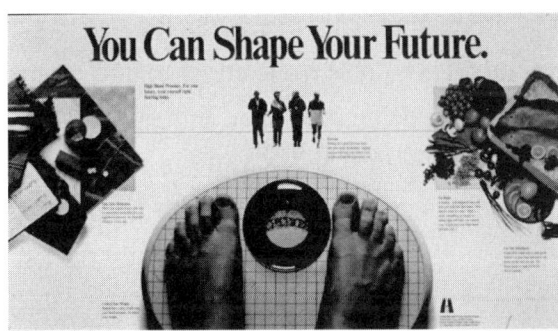

出典：VOA, Public Domain
http://ihm.nlm.nih.gov/

00:36-04:55

1   It is that time of year again! Warm weather has returned to Earth's northern hemisphere. Summer is a time when people of all ages feel like getting their swimwear and going to the nearest swimming pool or seashore. But first, there is that troublesome little thing called winter weight gain.

5   Many of us gain weight because of inactivity during the winter. Some people go to extremes to lose that extra weight before going to the beach. In the weight loss industry, there is never a lack of ideas about how to lose weight.

Consider the sleeping beauty diet, where you sleep your way to weight loss. You cannot eat if you are sleeping, or so the theory goes. Then there is the
10 tapeworm diet. The tapeworm is said to help people lose weight by eating the food that is stored in their stomach. But first you have to be willing to swallow the little creature. This may be more trouble than many people want.

Strange new diets, treatments and exercise programs arrive on the market every day. Each one promises to help people lose weight and get a beach beautiful
15 body. The weight loss industry takes in billions of dollars each year, and it is growing. One research company estimates the weight loss business will be worth

about $670 billion worldwide by the year 2015.

Markets and Markets says the business is made up of three major parts. They are weight loss services; physical fitness and surgical equipment; and diets, including foods and drinks. There is a seemingly endless supply of ideas about how to lose weight. There are low-carbohydrate diets and low-fat diets, diets that limit calories and ones that let you eat as much as you want. And, there are thousands of different kinds of diet pills and programs.

So where does one begin? Which one is best? Experts say there is no single diet plan that works best for everyone. Many experts agree on one thing: that to lose weight, you must use or burn off more calories than you take in. When you eat more calories than your body needs, it stores that extra energy as fat.

Calories are a measure of energy in food. A pound of fat is equal to 453 grams or about 3,500 calories. To lose that fat in a week, you have to burn off at least that amount in calories or eat that much less. The best thing to do is to combine both ideas. Eat fewer calories and increase physical activity so that you burn off more.

America's National Institutes of Health has suggested that women limit calories to no less than 1,200 calories a day without medical supervision. It also says men should have no less than 1,500 calories. Debate continues about the best way to fill those calories requirement.

| 読解のための語彙，文法および構文 |

（ナレーション後の音楽から）

p.1 ℓ.1 time of year: 時期，時節

p.1 ℓ.1 warm weather: 温暖な天気

p.1 ℓ.1-2 Earth's northern hemisphere: 北半球 【語源】hemi（半分）+ sphere（球体）

p.1 ℓ.2 feel like: ～したい（ような）気がする，～したい気分である

p.1 ℓ.2-3 getting their swimwear: 水着を着て

p.1 ℓ.3 seashore: 海辺，浜辺

p.1 ℓ.4 troublesome: 面倒な，厄介な，煩わしい

p.1 ℓ.4 winter weight gain: 冬期間の体重増加

p.1 ℓ.5 gain weight: 体重が増える，太る

p.1 ℓ.5 because of inactivity: 運動不足のため

p.1 ℓ.6 go to extremes: 極端に走る，極端なことをする

p.1 ℓ.6 to lose that extra weight: 余分な体重を減らすために

Unit 1　Losing Weight Proves to Be Big Business　*3*

p.1 ℓ.6-7	weight loss industry:	ダイエット産業
p.1 ℓ.7	never a lack of:	不足することがない
p.1 ℓ.8	sleeping beauty:	眠り姫，眠れる美女
p.1 ℓ.9	then:	それから
p.1 ℓ.10	tapeworm:	サナダムシ
p.1 ℓ.12	creature:	生物
p.1 ℓ.12	This may be more trouble:	これはもっと問題になるだろう．痩せたくてサナダムシのような寄生虫を飲むのは本末転倒であると著者は言いたいのである．
p.1 ℓ.13	strange:	奇妙な，変わった
p.1 ℓ.13	arrive on the market:	市場に出回る
p.1 ℓ.14-15	help people lose weight and get a beach beautiful body:	help A 動詞の原形 B で，A が B するのを手助けする．ここでは「人々が痩せて海岸で映える美しい肉体を手に入れるのを手助けする」という意味．
p.1 ℓ.15	takes in:	売り上げる，収益を得る
p.1 ℓ.15	billions of dollars:	数十億ドル，何十億ドル
p.1 ℓ.16	research company:	調査会社
p.1 ℓ.16	estimates:	見積もる，概算する
p.1 ℓ.16	weight loss business:	ダイエット・ビジネス
p.1 ℓ.16	be worth ：	〜の価値がある，〜の値打ちがある
p.2 ℓ.17	worldwide:	世界で
p.2 ℓ.18	Markets and Markets:	マーケット・アンド・マーケット
p.2 ℓ.18	is made up of:	(be　) 〜で構成されている．同じ意味のイディオムに be composed of がある．
p.2 ℓ.19	weight loss services:	減量サービス
p.2 ℓ.19	physical fitness:	フィジカル・フィットネス
p.2 ℓ.19	surgical equipment:	美容整形
p.2 ℓ.19	diets:	飲食物．日本語のカタカナのダイエットは英語の diet とは異なる意味で使われていることに注意．
p.2 ℓ.20	a seemingly endless supply of ideas:	アイデアは尽きることがないように見える
p.2 ℓ.21	low-carbohydrate diets:	炭水化物の少ない食事，低炭水化物ダイエット（炭水化物を徹底的に制限したダイエット方法．肉類は制限しない）．
p.2 ℓ.21	low-fat diets:	低脂肪食
p.2 ℓ.22	eat as much as you want:	食べたいだけ食べる
p.2 ℓ.23	diet pills:	痩せ薬

p.2 ℓ.24　experts: 専門家
p.2 ℓ.25　works best for everyone: あらゆる人に最適に作用する
p.2 ℓ.25　agree on: 同意している
p.2 ℓ.26　burn off: 燃焼させる，（カロリーを）消費させる
p.2 ℓ.26　take in: 摂取する
p.2 ℓ.27　it stores that extra energy as fat: 余計なエネルギーは脂肪として蓄えられる
p.2 ℓ.28　a measure of:（a　）～の尺度
p.2 ℓ.28　pound: ポンド．1ポンド＝453.592グラム
p.2 ℓ.28　equal to:（be　）～に等しい
p.2 ℓ.30　much less: もっと少なく
p.2 ℓ.33　America's National Institutes of Health: アメリカ国立衛生研究所（NIH）
　　　　【URL】http://www.nih.gov/
p.2 ℓ.34　medical supervision: 医学的管理
p.2 ℓ.34, 35　no less than　：～に劣らず，～と同じほど

Reading Comprehension Questions

次の各文が，本文の内容に合っていればTを，合っていない場合はFを，括弧内に記入してください．

1. (　) Experts say exercise alone is not enough if your goal is to lose weight.
2. (　) In Summer, a few people feel like getting their swimwear.
3. (　) A lot of people gain weight because of inactivity during the winter.
4. (　) Swallowing a little creature, tapeworm, may not be trouble.
5. (　) According to a research, by the year 2015, the weight loss business will be worth about $670 billion worldwide.
6. (　) There are thousands of different kinds of diet pills and programs for losing weight.
7. (　) Experts say there is single diet plan that works best for everyone.
8. (　) If you eat more calories than your body requires, it stores fat.
9. (　) Calories are a measure of energy other than food.
10. (　) Eating plans that contain 1,000 to 1,200 calories each day will help most women lose weight safely.

Listening Comprehension Questions

次の英語を聴いて空欄を埋めてください．

http://learningenglish.voanews.com/audio/audio/298267.html

00:02-00:28

(　　　) is Science in the (　　　　) in VOA Special English. I'm Shirley Griffith. And I'm Bob Doughty. (　　　　) we will talk about diet and weight loss. (　　　　　) is important if you want to get in good shape. But (　　　　　) say exercise alone is not enough if your goal is to lose (　　　　　).

English Composition

次の日本文を英文に直してください．

1. 温暖な気候が北半球に戻ってきた．（return を使って）

　

2. 私たちの多くが冬期間の運動不足のために体重が増える．（gain を使って）

　

3. ダイエット産業は毎年何十億ドルもの収益がある．（take in を使って）

ひとくちコラム

　アメリカの食べ物は「大きすぎ，糖分が多く不健康」と思い込む人は多い．『世界の食文化：アメリカXII』（本間千枝子ほか著，農山漁村文化協会，2004年）によると，アメリカの食文化史に現代の肥満を想起させる歴史はない．最近のアメリカのスーパーでは，有機栽培の野菜を販売し，カロリーや内容物を厳密に表示して健康に留意した食品が多く販売されている．現代病とも言われる肥満は，何が原因なのか．2010年，オバマ政権はファーストレディのミシェル・オバマ夫人を中心に，肥満対策を講じた．ダイエット産業は政府の肥満対策に便乗し，肥満に悩む人々をターゲットにし，莫大な利益をあげている．このダイエット産業はどこまで続くのか．今後も注目に値する産業である．

Unit 2

Environment

A Silent Killer – Carbon Monoxide Poisoning

http://learningenglish.voanews.com/a/2323013.html

出典：VOA, Public Domain
http://gdb.voanews.com/CE591346-5CB9-47E1-BBDD-34CF06D968BF_w640_r1_s_cx0_cy27_cw0.jpg

00:49-04:57

1   Two Chinese men were found dead in their hotel room in Nepal earlier this month. A medical expert spoke to Agence France-Presse after he had examined the bodies. The medical examiner blamed the deaths on carbon monoxide poisoning from a malfunctioning gas heater. A local police official said poor air
5 flow in the hotel room could have been partly responsible for the deaths.

   Also in December, police officers were called to a home in the American community of Commerce City, Colorado. They found one man dead and seven other people suffering from carbon monoxide poisoning. The seven were taken to a hospital for treatment.

10   These are just two of the cases of carbon monoxide poisoning that have been reported around the world this month. The United States' Centers for Disease Control and Prevention estimates that carbon monoxide kills hundreds of people every year, and sickens thousands.

   The CDC notes that carbon monoxide poisoning can happen outdoors in fresh
15 air. It says the gas has been linked with power-generating equipment and with engines on houseboats.

The Consumer Product Safety Commission is responsible for protecting Americans from unreasonable risks of death or injury from thousands of products. The commission studies death records and estimates the number of carbon monoxide-related deaths that could be linked to products under its supervision.

There were an estimated 146 such deaths in 2009 -- the most recent year for which information is available. The report says 53 percent of the deaths involved engine-driven tools, like generators. Heating systems were blamed for 27 percent of the deaths. The rest of the deaths were blamed on gases from charcoal grills, water heaters and lanterns.

Carbon monoxide poisoning is not only a problem in the United States. It causes many deaths and injuries to people and animals around the world. The gas has been a problem since people first began burning fuels to cook food or to create heat. It is a problem in all parts of the world that experience cold weather.

Carbon monoxide is called the silent killer because people do not know it is in the air. The gas has no color. It has no taste. It has no smell. It does not cause a burning sensation in the eyes. And it does not cause people to cough. But it can be deadly. It quickly robs the body of its ability to use oxygen.

Carbon monoxide decreases the ability of the blood to carry oxygen to body tissues. It does this by linking with the blood. When the gas links with the blood, the blood is no longer able to carry oxygen to the tissues that need it.

読解のための語彙，文法および構文

p.6 ℓ.1 **found dead in their hotel room**: ホテルの部屋で死亡しているのが発見された

p.6 ℓ.2 **medical expert**: 医師

p.6 ℓ.2 **Agence France-Presse**: フランス通信社，略語は AFP.【URL】http://www.afp.com/home/

p.6 ℓ.2-3 **examine the body**: 検視する

p.6 ℓ.3 **medical examiner**: 監察医，検視官

p.6 ℓ.3 **blame A on B**: A を B のせいにする

p.6 ℓ.3-4 **carbon monoxide poisoning**: 一酸化炭素中毒

p.6 ℓ.4 **malfunctioning**: 正常に機能しない

p.6 ℓ.4 **gas heater**: ガスストーブ

p.6 ℓ.4 **local police official**: 地元の警察（署）

p.6 ℓ.4-5 **poor air flow**: 悪い空気の流れ

p.6 ℓ.6 **police officers**: 警察官，巡査

p.6 ℓ.7	Commerce City:	商業都市
p.6 ℓ.7	Colorado:	コロラド州
p.6 ℓ.8	suffering from :	～に苦しむ
p.6 ℓ.8-9	were taken to a hospital for treatment:	治療のために病院に運ばれた
p.6 ℓ.11	reported around the world:	世界中で報告されている
p.6 ℓ.11-12	Centers for Disease Control and Prevention:	アメリカ疾病対策予防センター（略語はCDC）【URL】http://www.cdc.gov
p.6 ℓ.13	sicken:	病気にさせる，体調不良にする
p.6 ℓ.14	note:	注目する，指摘する，言及する
p.6 ℓ.14-15	fresh air:	外気，新鮮な空気
p.6 ℓ.15	power-generating equipment:	発電装置
p.6 ℓ.16	houseboats:	ハウスボート，宿泊設備付きヨット
p.7 ℓ.17	Consumer Product Safety Commission:	消費者製品安全委員会（略語はCPSC）【URL】http://www.cpsc.gov/
p.7 ℓ.18	unreasonable risks:	不当なリスク
p.7 ℓ.19	commission:	委員会
p.7 ℓ.20	under its supervision:	管理下で，監督下で
p.7 ℓ.21	the most recent year:	最近
p.7 ℓ.23	engine-driven tools:	エンジン駆動の道具
p.7 ℓ.23	generator:	発電機
p.7 ℓ.23	heating system:	暖房装置
p.7 ℓ.24	rest of:	他の
p.7 ℓ.24	charcoal grills:	木炭使用のグリル
p.7 ℓ.25	water heater:	温水器，給湯装置
p.7 ℓ.25	lantern:	ランタン，ちょうちん
p.7 ℓ.26	not only :	単に～のみならず，～だけでなく
p.7 ℓ.28	since :	～以来
p.7 ℓ.28	fuel:	燃料
p.7 ℓ.28	cook food:	食品を調理する
p.7 ℓ.29	cold weather:	寒い天候
p.7 ℓ.30	silent killer:	サイレントキラー
p.7 ℓ.31	in the air:	空中に，漂って
p.7 ℓ.31	no taste:	無味
p.7 ℓ.31	no smell:	無臭
p.7 ℓ.32	burning:	燃焼

p.7 ℓ.32	sensation:	感覚
p.7 ℓ.32	cough:	せき
p.7 ℓ.33	rob:	侵入する
p.7 ℓ.34	decreases the ability:	能力を低下させる
p.7 ℓ.34, 35, 36	blood:	血液
p.7 ℓ.34-35	carry oxygen to body tissues:	身体の組織に酸素を運ぶ
p.7 ℓ.35	link with the blood:	血中に入る

Reading Comprehension Questions

次の各文が，本文の内容に合っていればTを，合っていない場合はFを，括弧内に記入してください．

1. (　) A Chinese man was found dead in their hotel room in Nepal earlier this month.
2. (　) The medical examiner blamed the deaths on carbon monoxide poisoning.
3. (　) Police officers found one man dead and seven other people suffering from carbon monoxide poisoning.
4. (　) Centers for Disease Control and Prevention estimates that carbon dioxide kills hundreds of people every year
5. (　) The CDC notes that carbon monoxide poisoning can not happen outdoors in fresh air.
6. (　) The Consumer Product Safety Commission is responsible for protecting Americans from unreasonable risks of death or injury.
7. (　) There were an estimated 146 carbon monoxide-related deaths in 2009.
8. (　) Carbon monoxide poisoning does not cause many deaths and injuries to people and animals around the world.
9. (　) Carbon monoxide is called the silent killer.
10. (　) Carbon monoxide increases the ability of the blood to carry oxygen to body tissues.

Listening Comprehension Questions

次の英語を聴いて空欄を埋めてください．

http://learningenglish.voanews.com/audio/audio/358326.html

[00:02-00:30]

I'm Bob Doughty. And I'm June Simms. (　　　) (　　) (　　　) cold weather to many parts of Earth's northern (　　　). With the cold (　　) a danger as old as our knowledge of fire -- death or injury by (　　　) (　　　　) (　　　　). Today, we (　　) (　　) this ancient and continuing danger.

English Composition

次の日本文を英文に直してください．

1. 今月初めネパールのホテルの一室で2名の中国人男性が死亡しているのが発見された．（find を使って）

2. 7名が治療のために病院に運ばれた．（take を使って）

3. 一酸化炭素は血液が酸素を身体の組織に運ぶ能力を低下させる．（decrease を使って）

ひとくちコラム

「環境問題」では，地球温暖化との関連で二酸化炭素が話題になる頻度が多い．しかし「サイレント・キラー」と呼ばれる一酸化炭素は人類が火を起こすことを発見した太古の昔から人間に害をおよぼしてきた．一酸化炭素中毒に関し，各国政府，地方自治体の保健衛生担当部署がホームページ等を通じて他の疾病と紛らわしい症状を詳述し警告している．アメリカの場合は州の保健局等が担当している．日本では消防署が担当し，ホームページ上で注意を呼びかけている．

Unit 3　　　　Science and Technology

Scientific and Engineering Inventions Save Lives

http://learningenglish.voanews.com/a/2248894.html

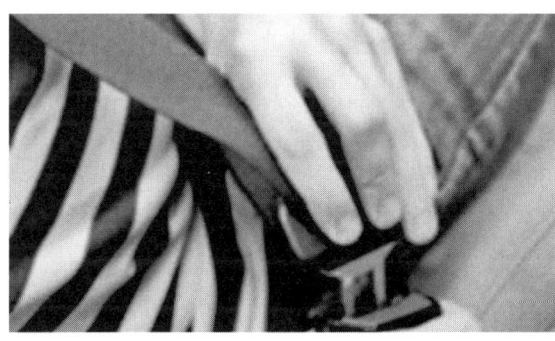

出典：VOA, Public Domain
http://gdb.voanews.com/A622704E-82CD-4616-B054-
77844BDAAD21_w640_r1_s.jpg

00:36-05:41

1　　Most cars have seat belts as part of their equipment. Seat belts protect drivers and passengers in case of accident. Safety experts estimate that the restraining devices save thousands of lives a year in the United States alone. Worldwide, some experts say, the devices have protected up to a million people.

5　　The first seat belt was said to have been created in the 1800s by George Cayley of England. He is remembered for many inventions, especially for early "flying machines."

　　The United States first recognized the invention of an automobile seat belt in 1849. The government gave a patent to Edward J. Claghorn of New York City 10 so that others would not copy his invention. Claghorn called the device a Safety-Belt. It was said to include hooks and other attachments for securing the person to a fixed object.

　　Other inventors followed with different versions of the seat belt. But more than 100 years passed before the current, widely used seat belt was developed. It 15 resulted from the work of a Swedish engineer, Nils Bohlin. His three-point, lap and shoulder seat belt first appeared on cars in Europe 50 years ago.

Bohlin was born in Sweden in 1920. After completing college, he designed seats for the Swedish aircraft industry. The seats were built for the pilot to escape from an airplane in case of disaster. Bohlin's work with planes showed him what could happen in a crash at high speed. In 1958, Bohlin brought that knowledge to the Swedish car manufacturer Volvo. He was the company's first chief safety engineer.

At the time, most safety belts in cars crossed the body over the abdomen. A buckle held the restraints in place. But the position of the buckle often caused severe injuries in bad crashes.

Nils Bohlin recognized that both the upper and lower body needed to be held securely in place. His invention contained a cloth strap that was placed across the chest and another strap across the hips. The design joined the straps next to the hip.

Volvo was the first automobile manufacturer to offer the modern seat belt as a permanent addition to its cars. It also provided use of Nils Bohlin's design to other car-makers.

The Swedish engineer won many honors for his seat belt. He received a gold medal from the Royal Swedish Academy of Engineering Sciences in 1995. He died in Sweden in 2002.

Kevlar is another invention that has saved many people from serious injury and death. Kevlar is a fibrous material with qualities that make it able to reject bullets. Added to clothing, the material protects security officers and soldiers across the world.

The fibers form a protective barrier against gunfire. Bullets lose their shape when they strike Kevlar. Those bullets look like mushrooms, and do not enter the body. Most threats to police and security officers come from handguns. They wear Kevlar vests to protect the upper body. Soldiers wear more extensive clothing protected with Kevlar against heavier ammunition.

読解のための語彙，文法および構文

タイトル	save lives:	命を救う
p.11 ℓ.6, 8, 10 p.12 ℓ.27, 36	invention:	発明（品），考案
p.11 ℓ.1	seat belts:	シートベルト
p.11 ℓ.1	equipment:	装置，機器
p.11 ℓ.1, 4 p.12 ℓ.38, 40, 43, 44	protect:	保護する

Unit 3 Scientific and Engineering Inventions Save Lives *13*

p.11 ℓ.1-2	drivers and passengers:	運転手と乗員
p.11 ℓ.2	in case of accident:	事故の場合
p.11 ℓ.2	safety experts:	安全に関する専門家
p.11 ℓ.2	estimate:	評価する，見積もる
p.11 ℓ.2-3	restraining devices:	拘束具
p.11 ℓ.3	worldwide:	世界中で，世界的には
p.11 ℓ.4	up to a million people:	最高で100万人
p.11 ℓ.5	was said to :	～と言われていた
p.11 ℓ.6	especially:	特に
p.11 ℓ.8	recognized:	認める，承認する
p.11 ℓ.8	automobile seat belt:	車のシートベルト
p.11 ℓ.9	give a patent to :	～に特許を付与する
p.11 ℓ.10	so that :	～となるように
p.11 ℓ.10	copy:	複製する
p.11 ℓ.4, 10	device:	装置
p.11 ℓ.11	It was said to :	～すると言われている
p.11 ℓ.11	attachments:	付属品
p.11 ℓ.11	secure:	固定する
p.11 ℓ.12	fixed object:	固定装置
p.11 ℓ.13	followed with :	～をさらに付け加える，～で続く
p.11 ℓ.13-14	more than 100 years passed before the current:	現在までに100年を超える年数が経った
p.11 ℓ.15	resulted from :	～のおかげで，～に起因する
p.11 ℓ.15 p.12 ℓ.33, 34	engineer:	技師，技術者
p.11 ℓ.15-16	three-point, lap and shoulder seat belt:	膝から肩までの三点を固定するシートベルト
p.12 ℓ.17	completing college:	大学を卒業する
p.12 ℓ.18	aircraft industry:	航空業界
p.12 ℓ.18	were built for:	製造された
p.12 ℓ.19	disaster:	災害
p.12 ℓ.20	a crash at high speed:	高速での衝突
p.12 ℓ.21	Swedish car manufacturer Volvo:	スウェーデンの車両メーカー，ボルボ
p.12 ℓ.21-22	chief safety engineer:	安全技術主任
p.12 ℓ.23	at the time:	当時
p.12 ℓ.23	over the abdomen:	腹部（の上）を

p.12 ℓ.24	buckle:	（ベルトの）バックル
p.12 ℓ.24	held the restraints in place:	所定の場所に固定する
p.12 ℓ.24-25	caused severe injuries in bad crashes:	酷い衝突の際は重傷の原因となった
p.12 ℓ.26-27	the upper and lower body needed to be held securely in place:	身体の上部と下部がしっかりと固定される必要があった
p.12 ℓ.27	cloth strap:	布製のストラップ
p.12 ℓ.28	chest:	胸部
p.12 ℓ.28	hips:	臀部
p.12 ℓ.28	next to ：	～の隣に，～に隣接して
p.12 ℓ.30	offer:	提供する
p.12 ℓ.31	permanent addition to ～:	～に常備された装置
p.12 ℓ.33	won many honors for his seat belt:	彼が製造したシートベルトで多くの名声を得た
p.12 ℓ.33-34	received a gold medal from:	金メダルを受賞した
p.12 ℓ.34	Royal Swedish Academy of Engineering Sciences:	スウェーデン王立科学アカデミー【URL】http://www.kva.se/
p.12 ℓ.36	Kevlar:	ケブラー． Kevlar vest は防弾チョッキ
p.12 ℓ.37	fibrous:	繊維状の，繊維
p.12 ℓ.37	material:	材質
p.12 ℓ.37-38	reject bullets:	弾丸をはねつける
p.12 ℓ.38	clothing:	衣類
p.12 ℓ.38	security officer:	公安警官
p.12 ℓ.38	soldier:	兵士
p.12 ℓ.39	across the world:	世界中で
p.12 ℓ.40	fibers:	繊維
p.12 ℓ.40	form:	形成する
p.12 ℓ.40	protective barrier:	保護的バリア
p.12 ℓ.40	gunfire:	銃撃
p.12 ℓ.41	look like ：	～のように見える
p.12 ℓ.41	mushroom(s)：	キノコ
p.12 ℓ.42	threat(s)：	脅威
p.12 ℓ.42	handgun(s)：	拳銃
p.12 ℓ.43	Kevlar vest(s)：	防弾チョッキ
p.12 ℓ.43	upper body:	上半身
p.12 ℓ.43	more extensive:	さらに広大な範囲で

p.12 ℓ.44   heavier ammunition: 重火器

Reading Comprehension Questions

次の各文が，本文の内容に合っていればTを，合っていない場合はFを，括弧内に記入してください．

1. (　) Most cars have seat belts as part of their equipment.
2. (　) The first seat belt was said to have been created in the 1800s by George Cayley of the United States.
3. (　) The United States first recognized the invention of an automobile in 1849.
4. (　) Nils Bohlin's three-point, lap and shoulder seat belt first appeared on cars in Europe 50 years ago.
5. (　) Bohlin was the first chief safety engineer of the Swedish car manufacturer Volvo.
6. (　) Most safety belts in cars crossing the body over the abdomen were safe even in bad crashes.
7. (　) Nils Bohlin recognized that both the upper and lower body needed to be held securely in place.
8. (　) Volvo was the first automobile manufacturer in the world.
9. (　) Volvo did not provide use of Nils Bohlin's design to other car-makers.
10. (　) Nils Bohlin won many honors for his seat belt.

Listening Comprehension Questions

次の英語を聴いて空欄を埋めてください．

http://learningenglish.voanews.com/audio/audio/283105.html

(00:01-00:22)

This is (　　　) in the News, in VOA Special English. I'm June Simms. Today Shirley Griffith and Bob Doughty (　　　) (　　　) two (　　　) (　　　) that (　　　) (　　　) to (　　　) (　　　). We will also tell about the people who (　　　) them.

English Composition

次の日本文を英文に直してください．

1. シートベルトは事故が起きると，運転手と乗員を守る．（protect を使って）
   _____

2. クレイグホーンはその装置を安全ベルトと名付けた．（call を使って）
   _____

3. 当時，最も安全な車のシートベルトは腹部で交差していた．（cross を使って）
   _____

ひとくちコラム

アメリカをはじめとして世界各国でシートベルトは着用が義務化されている．日本でも 2008 年から道路交通法が改正され，後部座席のシートベルト着用も義務化された．シートベルト非着用に対して反則金制度を導入している．ケブラーについては，防弾チョッキに使われる素材のため，日本では一般人にはなじみが薄いが，人命を守るために考案された素材である．いずれも科学技術を結集して作り上げた人命を保護するための貴重な装置，素材である．

Unit 4　　　　　　　　　　　　　　　　　　　　　　History

The American Civil War: Who Should Memorials Honor?

http://learningenglish.voanews.com/a/2230419.html

出典：VOA, Public Domain
http://learningenglish.voanews.com/content/article/1617448.html

00:49-04:54

1　　The Civil War was the bloodiest war in the history of the United States. From 1861 to 1865, at least 620,000 soldiers died in the fighting. It began after several southern states broke away from the North, mainly over the issue of slavery. The southern states declared independence and set up the Confederate States of
5 America, also known as the Confederacy. Now, 150 years later, a living memorial is being created to honor the war dead. Jim Tedder has more on the project.

　　The non-profit group Journey through Hallowed Ground is leading the effort. It plans to plant a tree, or recognize an existing tree, for each soldier killed in the war. The memorial will come to life along an almost 300 hundred kilometer road
10 that passes through four states. It will start in Gettysburg, Pennsylvania, where the most famous Civil War battle took place. It will end at the Charlottesville, Virginia, home of Thomas Jefferson, America's third president.

　　Beth Erickson is with Journey through Hallowed Ground. "As you see these trees, one after another, it will truly make an impact." The first trees were planted
15 in November on the grounds of a large, old Virginia home and farm called Oatlands. An historic trust now owns the former plantation.

Andrea McGimsey is the Executive Director of Oatlands. She says the former plantation was a good place to start. "Oatlands has some very old trees and they were here during the civil war time. Many of them are actually going to be adopted as part of the project." She adds that Oatlands is a part of Civil War history. "Oatlands had 128 slaves in 1860, right before the Civil War started. And also the family who lived here had two sons who joined the Confederate Army."

　　Richard Williams is a member of the last family to live at Oatlands. His family still owns property next to the home. And they are involved in planting the trees. "We're hoping that as private landowners we can also show it's a great success and encourage some other private landowners."

　　Private donations are expected to pay for the 65 million dollar tree planting project. The cost of an individual tree donation is 100 dollars. The trees will be especially interesting for Smart Phone users. Special markings on the trees can connect users with the stories of individual Civil War soldiers.

　　Beth Erickson explains. "These trees will be able to have a number associated with a person. They can use GPS technology to be able to find out who these people were."

　　Eleanor Adams has donated a tree in honor of her ancestor Joseph McGowan. He was from Alabama and fought for the South. He was 23 when he was shot and killed. Eleanor Adams says the young soldier wrote letters to his family about life on the battlefield. "He talks about sickness, the heat in the summertime, the bad food – really a tough time being a soldier in those days." She says she hopes other family members will join her in planting trees for other McGowans who died in the Civil War.

読解のための語彙，文法および構文

- タイトル memorials: 記念物
- タイトル honor: に敬意を払う
- p.17 ℓ.1　the Civil War: アメリカ南北戦争（1861 〜 1865 年）
- p.17 ℓ.1　bloodiest: 残忍な，悲惨な
- p.17 ℓ.2　at least: 少なくとも
- p.17 ℓ.2／p.18 ℓ.30　soldiers: 兵士
- p.17 ℓ.2　in the fighting: 戦争で
- p.17 ℓ.3　break away from: 〜とのつながりを断つ，〜から独立する
- p.17 ℓ.3　issue of slavery: 奴隷制の問題

Unit 4　The American Civil War: Who Should Memorials Honor?　*19*

p.17 ℓ.4	independence: 独立	
p.17 ℓ.4-5	set up the Confederate States of America: 南部連合国を作る	
p.17 ℓ.5	living memorial: 生きている記念物（ここでは植樹のこと）	
p.17 ℓ.6	honor the war dead: 南北戦争で亡くなった兵士を祀る	
p.17 ℓ.7	non-profit group: 非営利団体	
p.17 ℓ.7	leading the effort: その活動を先導する	
p.17 ℓ.8	plant a tree: 木を植える，植樹する	
p.17 ℓ.9	memorial: 記念物（ここでは記念樹）	
p.17 ℓ.9	road: 道路	
p.17 ℓ.10	passes through four states: 4州にまたがる	
p.17 ℓ.11	battle took place: 戦いが行われた	
p.17 ℓ.12	Thomas Jefferson: トマス・ジェファーソン．アメリカ第3代大統領（在任期間1801-09年）．フランスからルイジアナを買収した．欧州で起きたナポレオン戦争には不介入政策をとった．	
p.17 ℓ.14	one after another: 次々に	
p.17 ℓ.15	on the grounds of　: 〜の地に	
p.17 ℓ.16	historic trust: 歴史トラスト	
p.17 ℓ.16	former plantation: かつてのプランテーション	
p.18 ℓ.17	Executive Director: 常務理事，専務理事	
p.18 ℓ.19	actually: 実際に	
p.18 ℓ.20	adopt: 採用する	
p.18 ℓ.22	Confederate Army: 南軍（これに対して北軍は Union Army）	
p.18 ℓ.24	property: 所有地	
p.18 ℓ.25	landowner: 土地所有者	
p.18 ℓ.27	private donation: 個人の寄付	
p.18 ℓ.29	Smart Phone users: スマートフォンのユーザー	
p.18 ℓ.31-32	a number associated with a person: ひとりひとりに番号が割り当てられる	
p.18 ℓ.32	use GPS technology: GPS 機能を使う	
p.18 ℓ.34	in honor of: 敬意を表する	
p.18 ℓ.34	ancestor: 先祖	
p.18 ℓ.35	fought for the South: 南部のために戦った	
p.18 ℓ.37	battlefield: 戦場	
p.18 ℓ.37	heat in the summertime: 夏の暑さ	
p.18 ℓ.38	tough time being a soldier in those days: あのような時代に兵士になることは大変だった	

p.18 ℓ.39　join her in planting trees: 彼女の植樹（プロジェクト）に参加する

Reading Comprehension Questions

次の各文が，本文の内容に合っていればTを，合っていない場合はFを，括弧内に記入してください．

1. (　) The Civil War was the bloodiest war in the history of the United States.
2. (　) The Civil War began after several southern states broke away from the North.
3. (　) Hallowed Ground doesn't plan to plant a tree.
4. (　) West Virginia is home of Thomas Jefferson, America's third president.
5. (　) The first trees were planted in November on the grounds of Oatlands.
6. (　) Richard Williams' family are not involved in planting the trees.
7. (　) The cost of an individual tree donation is 100 dollars.
8. (　) The trees will be especially interesting for PC users.
9. (　) Joseph McGowan was 23 when he was shot and killed.
10. (　) Eleanor Adams doesn't hope other family members will join planting trees.

Listening Comprehension Questions

次の英語を聴いて空欄を埋めてください．
http://learningenglish.voanews.com/audio/audio/264408.html

[00:04-00:39]

(　　　　) to AMERICAN MOSAIC, in VOA Special English. I'm June Simms. On the show today, we (　　　) music from some of the performers at the South by Southwest music festival in Austin, Texas. We (　　　) (　　　) efforts to (　　　　) the many Americans (　　　) in the nation's Civil War in the 1860s. And we (　　　) (　　　) efforts against some of the Civil War memorials that already (　　　).

English Composition

次の日本文を英文に直してください.

1. 少なくとも 62 万人の兵士がその戦争で死亡した.（die を使って）

   _____

2. 南部の州は独立を宣言した.（declare を使って）

   _____

3. 植樹プロジェクトに対する民間の寄付は 6,500 万ドルが期待されている.（be expected を使って）

   _____

ひとくちコラム

"civil war" には,「内戦」という意味がある. アメリカ史上で内戦があったのは, 南北戦争だけである. 南北戦争は北部のアメリカ合衆国と, 合衆国から脱退した南部の南部連合国の奴隷制度をめぐる対立が原因の一つであった. 第 16 代大統領エイブラハム・リンカーンによる有名な "government of the people, by the people, for the people"「人民の人民による人民のための政治」は, 1863 年に南北戦争の激戦地となったペンシルバニア州ゲティスバーグで開催された国立戦没者墓地の短い式典の際に語られた. 民主主義の本質を語った言葉である.

Unit 5　　　　　　　　　　　　　　　　　　　　Agriculture

Farmer Invents New Way to Grow Crops

http://learningenglish.voanews.com/a/2254636.html

出典：Wikipedia Commons, Public Domain
http://commons.wikimedia.org/wiki/File:Hrushikesh_kulkarni_vegetables.JPG

00:29-04:22

1　　Blake Whisenant and his family are farmers. They live in the American state of Florida. For nearly 100 years, Mr. Whisenant's family has grown fruits and vegetables, and sold them to businesses around the world. The warm weather in central Florida is good for growing crops, especially tomatoes. That is what he
5 grows the most of on his eight hundred hectares of land.

　　In 1992, Mr. Whisenant had some bad luck. It began to rain. And…it rained. And it rained some more. Nearly 50 centimeters of rain destroyed the tomato crop that year. Blake Whisenant was not a happy farmer.

　　"I just thought there's got to be a better way!" So, he began looking to find a
10 way to make sure this never happened again. He wanted to develop a system that would provide water to the plants from below. He thought some kind of cover would keep rain away and the soil warm. He wanted the plants to be grown in a box that would take up little space. He became obsessed with the idea and thought about it day and night.

15　　"And I told my wife, before I die I wanted to see if I could build me a box above the ground that I could grow tomatoes in." And…after years of work…he knew what to do.

He found a company in Pennsylvania that agreed to make the box. It would be made of thick plastic, and would be about one meter long and half a meter deep. Inside the box would be a plastic tube to pour the water in, and a plastic screen with many holes in it.

Something like peat moss, but not soil, would be placed in the box on top of the screen, which would hold it above the water in the bottom of the box. A thin plastic cover would fit over the top of the box to keep out rain and harmful insects. Blake called it…the EarthBox.

Frank DiPaolo is the general manager of the EarthBox Company in Scranton, Pennsylvania. He says that growing vegetables this way…container gardening some call it…makes it easy for Blake Whisenant and other farmers to quickly solve common growing problems.

"When he saw any sort of disease or problems with the plants in the field, one human being could basically go and grab the box and just pull that problem right out of the field before it spread to the other plants."

Frank DiPaolo says normal dirt or soil will not work in this kind of container gardening. Instead, potting mix is used. This is mostly peat moss with a few things added to help air get to the roots of the plants.

"One of its responsibilities is to wick the water up to the plants. When you put a small seedling in, the roots are not deep enough to go into that water reservoir, so we need to bring the water up to the plant."

読解のための語彙，文法および構文

p.22 ℓ.1, 8
p.23 ℓ.28 **farmer(s)**：農業経営者，農場主，農業従事者．アメリカの場合は大規模な農場（farm）を営んでいる人も多くいる．

p.22 ℓ.1-2 **state of Florida:** フロリダ州

p.22 ℓ.2 **nearly 100 years:** 100年近く

p.22 ℓ.2-3 **fruits and vegetables:** 果物と野菜

p.22 ℓ.3 **businesses:** businessが可算名詞の場合は「企業」を指すことが多い．ここでは"businesses around the world"で世界中の企業のこと．

p.22 ℓ.4 **(be) good for** ：〜するのに良い

p.22 ℓ.4, 7 **crop(s)**：農作物

p.22 ℓ.4	That is what	：それが what 以下の〜である．前の文章を受けている．That はトマト栽培のこと．
p.22 ℓ.6	had some bad luck	：ある不運に見舞われた．（参照："have good luck"―幸運に恵まれる）
p.22 ℓ.6, 7	rain	: 雨が降る
p.22 ℓ.7	nearly	: だいたい，ほぼ
p.22 ℓ.7	destroy	: 台無しにする
p.22 ℓ.9	better way	: もっと良い方法
p.22 ℓ.9	look to	: 関心を向ける
p.22 ℓ.9-10	find a way	: 方法を見つける
p.22 ℓ.10	make sure	: 確認する
p.22 ℓ.10	develop	: 開発する
p.22 ℓ.11	provide water	: 水を供給する
p.22 ℓ.11	from below	: 下から
p.22 ℓ.12	keep rain away and the soil warm	: 雨を防いで土壌をあたためる
p.22 ℓ.13	take up little space	: ほとんど場所をとらない
p.22 ℓ.13	He became obsessed	: obsess は他動詞で「強迫観念となる」の意味になる．be, become などとともに受動態の形で「頭から離れない」という意味でも使われる．課題の場合は受動態で使われている．
p.22 ℓ.15	before I die	:「死ぬ前に」であるが，ここでは「死ぬまでに」と訳すと良い．
p.23 ℓ.16	after years of work	: 何年も取り組んだ後
p.23 ℓ.18-19	be made of	：（材料）〜で作られている
p.23 ℓ.20	inside the box	: 箱の中に
p.23 ℓ.20	plastic tube	: プラスチックの管
p.23 ℓ.20	pour the water in	: 水を注ぐ
p.23 ℓ.20	plastic screen	: プラスチックスクリーン
p.23 ℓ.22	peat moss	: ピートモス，ミズゴケ，草炭，泥炭コケ
p.23 ℓ.22, 33	soil	: 土
p.23 ℓ.22	(be) placed in the box	: 箱のなかに置かれた
p.23 ℓ.23	in the bottom of the box	: 箱の底部に
p.23 ℓ.24	fit over the top of the box	: 箱の上部にぴったりおさまる
p.23 ℓ.24-25	keep out rain and harmful insects	: 雨や害虫が入らないようにする
p.23 ℓ.25	call	: 〜と呼ぶ
p.23 ℓ.26	general manager	: 統括マネジャー，部長
p.23 ℓ.27	grow vegetables	: 野菜を栽培する

Unit 5　Farmer Invents New Way to Grow Crops　25

p.23 ℓ.29　　solve: 解決する
p.23 ℓ.30　　sort of: いわば，いわゆる
p.23 ℓ.30　　in the field: 田畑で
p.23 ℓ.31　　human being: 人間
p.23 ℓ.31　　basically: 基本的に
p.23 ℓ.31　　grab: 取り組む
p.23 ℓ.31-32　right out of: そのまま抜け出る
p.23 ℓ.32　　spread　：〜に広がる
p.23 ℓ.33　　dirt: 泥
p.23 ℓ.34　　instead: 代わりに
p.23 ℓ.34　　potting mix: 鉢植え用のミックスした土
p.23 ℓ.34-35　peat moss with a few things added to help air get to the roots of the plants: 作物の根に空気を取り込みやすくするために添加物を施したピートモス
p.23 ℓ.36　　to wick the water up to the plants: 作物に水を供給する．"wick" には "convey"「運ぶ」の意味がある．植物に給水すること．
p.23 ℓ.37　　seedling: 苗，苗木
p.23 ℓ.36-37　put in　：〜の中に入れる，〜に収納する
p.23 ℓ.37　　reservoir: 容器

Reading Comprehension Questions

次の各文が，本文の内容に合っていればTを，合っていない場合はFを，括弧内に記入してください．

1. (　) Blake Whisenant and his family are not farmers.
2. (　) In 1992, Blake Whisenant was not a happy farmer.
3. (　) He thought some kind of cover would keep rain away and the soil warm.
4. (　) Evern after years of work, Whisenant did not find what to do.
5. (　) He found a company in Pennsylvania that agreed to make the box.
6. (　) Something like peat moss, which was soil, would be placed in the box.
7. (　) Frank DiPaolo is the general manager of the EarthBox Company in Scranton.
8. (　) Disease or problems with the plants in the field are spread to the other plants.

9. (　　) Frank DiPaolo says normal dirt or soil will work in the container gardening.
10. (　　) One of the container gardening's responsibilities is to wick the water up to the plants.

Listening Comprehension Questions

次の英語を聴いて空欄を埋めてください．

http://learningenglish.voanews.com/audio/audio/288951.html

[00:00-00:22]

From VOA Learning English, this is (　　　　) in the News. (　　　　), we (　　　) (　　　) an American farmer and an unusual device he (　　　　). For (　　) years, people around the world (　　) (　　) (　　　) his (　　　　).

English Composition

次の日本文を英文に直してください．

1. 1992年，ウィズナント氏は不運に見舞われた．（have を使って）

2. 彼は，ペンシルバニア州でボックスを作ることに賛同してくれる会社を見つけた．（find, agree を使って）

3. ブレイクはそれをアースボックスと呼んだ．（call を使って）

ひとくちコラム

　アメリカは世界有数の農産物輸出国である．大部分が温帯に属しているが，ハワイ州，フロリダ州は熱帯，アラスカ州は寒帯とバラエティに富んだ気候に属しているため，さまざまな農産物を収穫することができる．日本の農林水産省(2013年9月)によると，アメリカは，とうもろこし，大豆，小麦等の穀物や畜産業が盛んである．特に穀物ではとうもろこし（年間3億1,395万トン），大豆（年間8,419万トン）が世界第1位の生産量を誇っている．課題のように農作物の生育方法にも気候に合わせた工夫がなされている．

Unit 6
Finance

For a New Nation, Hamilton Seeks a Bank

http://learningenglish.voanews.com/a/2310069.html

出典：VOA, Public Domain
http://gdb.voanews.com/A8C5A860-3B91-462D-8480-1B9AB35444FC_mw1024_n_s.jpg

00:36-05:10

1   Alexander Hamilton firmly believed that no country could become a modern nation without industry. So, he carefully developed a program that would make the United States an industrial nation.

   Part of his program protected American manufacturers from foreign
5 competition. Hamilton protected them by establishing a system of import taxes on some foreign goods brought into American ports. These tariffs raised the prices of those goods. As a result, American manufacturers had much less competition in selling their products.

   Alexander Hamilton also organized the nation's finances. One of his first steps
10 was to pay back the debt the country owed from the Revolutionary War. But Hamilton wanted to go much further. He wanted to establish a national bank.

   Hamilton argued that many European countries had national banks. University of Virginia history professor Andrew O'Shaughnessy says Hamilton saw the advantage of Britain's system. It permitted a very small country to go deeply into
15 debt while fighting wars.

   "The British had essentially been able to project power well beyond their size, thanks to a very efficient financial system and system of borrowing." Hamilton said a national bank in America would increase the flow of money throughout the

country. It would help the national government negotiate loans and collect taxes.
20 Business historian John Steele Gordon says Hamilton believed a centralized bank would also keep the states from competing with each other.

"Banks always have the problem that they're in the money business, so they're always tempted to lend too much and speculate too much. So he wanted a central mechanism to keep them on a short leash."

25 But Hamilton's plan raised old fears, especially among farmers in the South. Critics argued that a national bank would give too much power to a few rich men in the North. It would take control of state banks, on which southern farmers and small businessmen depended. It would also increase the use of paper money, instead of gold and silver.

30 James Madison led the opposition against Hamilton's plan in Congress. Madison said the United States should not put all its wealth in one place. So he proposed a system of many smaller banks in different parts of the country. He also argued that the idea of a central bank was unconstitutional.

No one knew more about the American Constitution than James Madison. He
35 was given credit for most of the ideas in it. Everyone respected his explanations of its wording.

Madison noted that the Constitution gave Congress a number of powers, which were stated. For example, the Constitution gave Congress the power to borrow money. But Congress could borrow money only to repay debts, to defend
40 the country and to provide for the general good of the people. Madison said permitting Congress to do more than what was in the Constitution was dangerous.

■ 読解のための語彙，文法および構文

p.27 ℓ.1　Alexander Hamilton: アレクサンダー・ハミルトン（1755年〜1804年—アメリカの政治学者であり，初代財務長官）．

p.27 ℓ.1　firmly believe　:〜を固く信じる

p.27 ℓ.1-2　modern nation: 近代国家

p.27 ℓ.2　industry: 工業

p.27 ℓ.2　program: 計画—ここではハミルトンのアメリカを工業国にする計画のこと．

p.27 ℓ.3　industrial nation: 工業国

p.27 ℓ.4　manufacturer: 製造業者

p.27 ℓ.5　competition: 競争

p.27 ℓ.5　protected: 保護する

Unit 6　For a New Nation, Hamilton Seeks a Bank

p.27 ℓ.5-6	import taxes on some foreign goods:	外国製品に課す輸入税
p.27 ℓ.6	tariff:	関税
p.27 ℓ.7	as a result:	結果として
p.27 ℓ.7-8	in selling their products:	自分たちの製品を販売する際は
p.27 ℓ.9	organize:	体系化する
p.27 ℓ.9	nation's finances:	国家財政
p.27 ℓ.10	pay back the debt:	負債を返済する
p.27 ℓ.10	the country owed from the Revolutionary War:	この"owe"は自動詞で「負債がある」で，"from the Revolutionary War"は「独立戦争時から」の意味である．
p.27 ℓ.11	go much further:	（計画を）さらに推し進める
p.27 ℓ.11	establish a national bank:	国立銀行を設立する
p.27 ℓ.12-13	University of Virginia:	バージニア大学　【URL】http://www.virginia.edu/ history
p.27 ℓ.13	professor Andrew O'Shaughnessy:	アンドリュー・オショネシー歴史学教授
p.27 ℓ.14-15	go deeply into debt:	多額の借金をする，多額の負債を負う
p.27 ℓ.16	project:	提案する，企画する
p.27 ℓ.16	well beyond　:	～よりはるかに優れて
p.27 ℓ.17	thanks to　:	～のおかげで
p.27 ℓ.17	borrowing:	借り入れ
p.27 ℓ.18	flow of money:	金の流れ
p.27 ℓ.18	throughout　:	～のいたるところで
p.28 ℓ.19	help the national government negotiate　:	～を交渉するのを支援する
p.28 ℓ.19	loans:	融資，借款
p.28 ℓ.19	collect taxes:	税金を取り立てる，徴税する
p.28 ℓ.20	business historian John Steele Gordon:	経営史家ジョン・スティール・ゴードン氏
p.28 ℓ.20	centralized bank:	中央銀行
p.28 ℓ.21	keep from:	避ける，回避する
p.28 ℓ.22-23	be tempted to　:	～する気になる
p.28 ℓ.23	lend too much:	多額を貸しすぎる
p.28 ℓ.23	speculate too much:	大金を投機しすぎる
p.28 ℓ.24	on leash:	紐で縛って，ここでは上記の傾向を抑えること，つまり「規制する」意味で使っている．
p.28 ℓ.25	among farmers in the South:	南部の農民の間で
p.28 ℓ.26	critics:	批評家
p.28 ℓ.26-27	a few rich men in the North:	北部の少数の富裕層
p.28 ℓ.27	take control:	統制する

p.28 ℓ.27 **state banks**: 州立銀行

p.28 ℓ.28 **small businessmen**: 中小企業家

p.28 ℓ.28 **paper money**: 紙幣，小切手

p.28 ℓ.29 **gold and silver**: 金や銀

p.28 ℓ.30 **James Madison**: ジェームズ・マディソン

p.28 ℓ.30 **Congress**: 議会

p.28 ℓ.31 **propose**: 提案する

p.28 ℓ.33 **unconstitutional**: 違憲の，憲法に反する．

p.28 ℓ.34 **American Constitution**: アメリカ合衆国憲法

p.28 ℓ.35 **be given credit for**　：〜の功績を認められる，〜で称賛される

p.28 ℓ.37 **noted**: 注目する ＝ pay attention

p.28 ℓ.37 **powers**: 権力

p.28 ℓ.39 **repay**: 返済する

p.28 ℓ.40 **provide for**　：〜に備える

p.28 ℓ.40 **general good**: 一般財

p.28 ℓ.40 **people**: 国民

Reading Comprehension Questions

次の各文が，本文の内容に合っていればＴを，合っていない場合はＦを，括弧内に記入してください．

1. (　　) Alexander Hamilton firmly believed that a country could become a modern nation without industry.
2. (　　) Part of Hamilton's program protected American manufacturers from foreign competition.
3. (　　) Hamilton organized the nation's finances.
4. (　　) According to professor Andrew O'Shaughnessy, Hamilton did not see the advantage of Britain's system
5. (　　) Hamilton said a national bank in America would increase the flow of money throughout the country.
6. (　　) Banks always have the problem that they're always tempted to lend too little and speculate too little.
7. (　　) Critics argued that a national bank would give too much power to a few rich men in the North.
8. (　　) James Madison did not lead the opposition against Hamilton's plan in Congress.

9. (　　) Everyone knew more about the American Constitution than James Madison.

10. (　　) Madison paid attention that the Constitution gave Congress a number of powers,

Listening Comprehension Questions

次の英語を聴いて空欄を埋めてください．

http://learningenglish.voanews.com/audio/audio/345315.html

[00:10-00:35]

From VOA Learning English, welcome to The (　　　) of a (　　　) – (　　　) (　　　) in VOA Special English. I'm Steve Ember. (　　　) (　　　) in our series we (　　　) the story of Alexander Hamilton. He was the nation's (　　　) (　　　) of the (　　　).

English Composition

次の日本文を英文に直してください．

1. ハミルトンは，アメリカを工業国にする計画を慎重に発展させた．（develop を使って）

2. ハミルトンはまた国家の財政を体系づけた．（organize を使って）

3. マディソンは，アメリカ合衆国は一箇所に富を集中するべきではないと述べた．（put all its wealth in を使って）

ひとくちコラム

アレクサンダー・ハミルトンは，初代アメリカ大統領ジョージ・ワシントン内閣で初代財務長官を務めた．アメリカ合衆国建国に関わった政治家である．財務長官としてアメリカ合衆国初の中央銀行を設立した．アメリカの連邦制導入是非をめぐる85編の論文を集めた『フェデラリスト（The Federalist Papers）』を執筆している．また，弁護士や実務家の資格も持ち，政界を退いた後もアメリカ合衆国の政治に多大な影響を及ぼした．最後は名誉毀損に関する事件でジェファーソン政権の副大統領であったアーロン・バーと決闘し，銃弾に倒れ，死亡した．

Unit 7

Government Politics

President Adams Avoids War with France

http://learningenglish.voanews.com/a/2240316.html

出典：VOA, Public Domain
http://gdb.voanews.com/B2B51850-6A88-4CBE-8D2A-9753DF7A0F05_mw1024_n_s.jpg

[00:48-05:29]

1   Adams was an intelligent man. He was a patriot and an able diplomat. But he did not like party politics. This dislike caused trouble during his presidency because two political parties struggled for power during his time in office. Adams was caught in the middle.

5   John Adams was a member of the Federalist Party. As president, he should have been party leader. But this position belonged to a man who really knew how to get and use political power, Alexander Hamilton.

     Hamilton had served as treasury secretary under President Washington. Now, Hamilton was a private citizen, a lawyer in New York City. But he continued to
10 have great influence over the national government. Federalists loyal to Hamilton controlled the Congress.

Even President Adams' top cabinet secretaries were loyal to Hamilton. In fact, they worked together against the new president. This political situation made Adams' term in office very difficult. It also led to the end of Federalist Party power.

John Ferling is a professor emeritus of history at the University of West Georgia. He has written many books about early American history. He says every 50 years or so the country experiences a period of extreme partisanship. He says the late 1700s were such a time. That partisanship helped split the Federalist Party.

"It was a group under Hamilton who were called the ultra-federalists, or the high federalists, at the time that were making war on the centrists. In their case it resulted really in the destruction of the Federalist Party. They never were a viable party again after the election of 1800."

Two major issues marked Adams' presidency. One concerned foreign policy. The other concerned the rights of citizens. The first involved America's relations with France. Americans were divided on whether to support the revolution in France. At first, many saw it as similar to the American Revolution against Britain. Vice President Thomas Jefferson, especially, supported the French.

France helped America win its war for independence from Britain. The countries' friendship continued when Thomas Jefferson served as minister to Paris.

But many Federalists came to strongly oppose the revolution in France. They were horrified by the execution of the French king and queen. They did not like the idea of common people taking power. Federalists wanted an alliance with Britain. Over time, they demanded war with France. They used their power to prevent the American government from sending a pro-French representative to Paris. They also searched for any signs of insult, any excuse to declare war.

John Ferling says President Adams did not agree with the majority of Federalists. "Adams, from the very beginning, seeks what he called an honorable peace. He tried to look for some sort of central position, centrist position, between the radical conservatives on the right and the radical liberals on the left."

読解のための語彙，文法および構文

p.32 ℓ.1 **Adams: John Adams.** ジョン・アダムズ（1735～1826年）アメリカ第2代大統領（1797～1801年）.

p.32 ℓ.1 **intelligent man:** 聡明な人間

p.32 ℓ.1 **patriot:** 愛国者

p.32 ℓ.1 **able diplomat:** 有能な外交官

p.32 ℓ.2   party politics: 政党政治

p.32 ℓ.2   presidency:（大統領の）任期

p.32 ℓ.3   struggled for ：〜のために闘った

p.32 ℓ.4   in the middle: 真っ只中

p.32 ℓ.5   Federalist Party:「連邦党」または「フェデラリスト」．この政党は 1789 年に初代財務長官のアレクサンダー・ハミルトンを中心として結成された政党である．

p.32 ℓ.6   party leader: 党首

p.32 ℓ.8   served as treasury secretary: 財務長官を務めた

p.32 ℓ.8   President Washington: ワシントン大統領．ジョージ・ワシントン（George Washington:1732 〜 1799 年）はアメリカ初代大統領（1789 〜 1797 年）．"the Father of his Country（建国の父）" と呼ばれる．

p.32 ℓ.9   private citizen: 一般市民

p.32 ℓ.9   lawyer: 弁護士

p.32 ℓ.10   loyal to: 〜に忠実な，〜派の

p.32 ℓ.11   Congress: 議会

p.33 ℓ.12   top cabinet secretaries: 閣僚

p.33 ℓ.12   In fact: 実際は

p.33 ℓ.14   Adams' term in office: 在任期間

p.33 ℓ.15   John Ferling: ジョン・ファーリング

p.33 ℓ.15   professor emeritus: 名誉教授

p.33 ℓ.15   University of West Georgia: ウエスト・ジョージア大学

p.33 ℓ.17   extreme partisanship:「党派心」とは 1 つの党派だけに偏る心．自分の仲間だけと親しくすること．

p.33 ℓ.19   ultra-federalists:「ウルトラ・フェデラリスト」

p.33 ℓ.20   high federalists:「ハイ・フェデラリスト」

p.33 ℓ.20   at the time: 当時は

p.33 ℓ.20   make war on ：〜を攻撃する，争う

p.33 ℓ.20   centrists: 中道主義者

p.33 ℓ.21   destruction: 破壊，崩壊

p.33 ℓ.21   viable: 存続可能な

p.33 ℓ.22   election of 1800: 1800 年に実施された選挙

p.33 ℓ.23   major issues: 大きな問題

p.33 ℓ.23   foreign policy: 外交

p.33 ℓ.24   rights of citizens: 市民権

p.33 ℓ.25   divide: 分裂する

- p.33 ℓ.25　revolution: 革命
- p.33 ℓ.26-27　American Revolution against Britain: イギリスに対して行ったアメリカの独立革命．独立戦争ともいう．
- p.33 ℓ.27　Vice President: 副大統領
- p.33 ℓ.27　Thomas Jefferson: トマス・ジェファーソン
- p.33 ℓ.28　independence: 独立
- p.33 ℓ.29　minister to Paris: フランス駐在大使．フランスの首都パリに政府が置かれているため，Paris でフランス政権を意味する場合もある．"minister" は大使の意味である．
- p.33 ℓ.30　oppose: 反対する
- p.33 ℓ.31　horrify: 怖がらせる
- p.33 ℓ.31　execution: 処刑
- p.33 ℓ.31　French king and queen: フランス王と女王
- p.33 ℓ.32　common people: 一般大衆
- p.33 ℓ.32　taking power: 権力（政権）を握る，掌握する
- p.33 ℓ.32　alliance: 同盟，協力関係
- p.33 ℓ.33　over time: やがて
- p.33 ℓ.33　prevent: 防ぐ
- p.33 ℓ.34　pro-French representative: フランス支持の代表
- p.33 ℓ.35　search for: 探す
- p.33 ℓ.35　insult: 侮辱
- p.33 ℓ.36　majority: 大多数
- p.33 ℓ.37　honorable peace: 名誉ある講和
- p.33 ℓ.38　look for: 探す，期待する
- p.33 ℓ.38　centrist: 中道
- p.33 ℓ.38-39　radical conservatives: 急進的な保守派
- p.33 ℓ.39　radical liberals: 急進的な自由主義者

Reading Comprehension Questions

次の各文が，本文の内容に合っていればTを，合っていない場合はFを，括弧内に記入してください．

1. (　　) Adams was not an intelligent man.
2. (　　) John Adams was a member of the Federalist Party.

3. (　　) Hamilton had served as treasury secretary under President Thomas Jefferson.
4. (　　) Even President Adams' top cabinet secretaries were loyal to Hamilton.
5. (　　) John Ferling has written a lot of books about early American history.
6. (　　) A group under Hamilton were not called the ultra-federalists.
7. (　　) Americans were divided on whether to support the revolution in France.
8. (　　) France did not help America win its war for independence from Britain.
9. (　　) Many Federalists came to strongly agree with the revolution in France.
10. (　　) President Adams did not agree with the majority of Federalists.

Listening Comprehension Questions

次の英語を聴いて空欄を埋めてください．

http://learningenglish.voanews.com/audio/audio/274427.html

(00:10-00:44)

From VOA Learning English, welcome to The Making of a Nation. American history in Special English. I'm Steve Ember. This week in our series, we (　　　　) the (　　　) of America's second president, John Adams. He (　　　) (　　　) in (　　　). He (　　) (　　　) eight years as vice president under President (　　　) (　　　). Now, state electors had chosen him to (　　　) the new nation.

English Composition

次の日本文を英文に直してください．

1. アダムズは政党政治が好きではなかった．（like を使って）

2. ハミルトンはワシントン大統領の下で財務長官として奉職した．（serve を使って）

3. アメリカ人はフランスで起きた革命を支持するか否かで分裂した．（divide を使って）

> **ひとくちコラム**
>
> アメリカ大統領の歴代大統領のなかで，2組の親子が大統領に就任している．第2代ジョン・アダムズ大統領（在任 1797－1801）と第6代ジョン・Q・アダムズ大統領（在任 1825－1829）の親子と，第41代ジョージ・ブッシュ大統領（在任 1989－1993）と第43代ジョージ・W・ブッシュ大統領（在任 2001－2009）の親子である．アダムズ大統領は右派と左派の間で中道主義を進めた穏健派と言われ，当時開戦の危機にあったフランスとの平和的解決を模索した．アメリカ海軍創設者でもある．

Unit 8

Poverty

U.S. Poverty Rate Highest Since 1993

http://learningenglish.voanews.com/a/1979821.html

出典：VOA, Public Domain
http://learningenglish.voanews.com/content/us-poverty-rate-highest-since-1993-129992358/130984.htm

(00:38-04:23)

1 　The American recession lasted from December of two thousand seven to June of two thousand nine. Since two thousand seven, the poverty rate has increased more than two and a half percentage points. The new findings did come as a surprise to Michael Ferrell of the Coalition for the Homeless in Washington, DC.

5 　MICHAEL FERRELL: "Unless there's a turnaround within the economy in the very near future, it's most likely to get worse."

　The Census Bureau says median household income fell more than two percent from two thousand nine to two thousand ten. Median means half earned more and half earned less. Last year, the median income was about forty-nine thousand
10 dollars.

　The Census Bureau says more than forty-six million people were living in poverty. It was the largest number since estimates began in nineteen fifty-nine. They included more than one-fourth of blacks and Hispanics, twelve percent of Asians and about ten percent of non-Hispanic whites.

15 　Some economic measures were unchanged. Women in full-time, year-round

jobs continued to earn an average of seventy-seven percent as much as men did. The number of people without health insurance rose from forty-nine million to almost fifty million last year. But the rate -- 16.3 percent -- was about the same as in two thousand nine.

Most Americans who have health insurance get it through their employers. Elise Gould at the Economic Policy Institute says people age eighteen to twenty-four are the least likely to get insurance plans through their employers. But she says young people are facing fewer barriers because of the nation's new health care law.

ELISE GOULD: "Health reform played a key role in stemming the fall of workplace coverage for young adults. The Patient Protection and Affordable Care Act, commonly known as health reform, included provisions that allowed young adults up to age twenty-six to secure health insurance coverage through their parents' employer-sponsored health insurance policies."

Experts say the biggest driving force of poverty is unemployment. About fourteen million Americans are unemployed. Millions more have stopped looking for work or wish they could work more hours.

Las Vegas, Nevada, is famous for its casinos and hotels. But the city was hit hard by the recession and the housing market crash that helped cause it. Former construction worker Richard Scanlon is disabled, but he says many able-bodied friends are out of work.

RICHARD SCANLON: "Ten, fifteen years ago, if you couldn't get a job in Vegas, you weren't looking for one. Now it's tough."

Family Promise is a national group that helps people get jobs and housing. Director Terry Lindemann says Family Promise of Las Vegas works with religious organizations that offer short-term housing.

読解のための語彙，文法および構文

- タイトル　U.S. Poverty Rate: アメリカの貧困水準，貧困率
- p.38 ℓ.2　poverty: アメリカでは, 貧困家庭とは「4人家族で年間所得または収入が2万2,300ドル未満の世帯」を言う.
- p.38 ℓ.1　recession: 景気後退，不景気
- p.38 ℓ.1　lasted from A to B: AからBまで続く
- p.38 ℓ.2　poverty rate: 貧困水準，貧困率
- p.38 ℓ.3　more than two and a half percentage points: 2.5 パーセント超. 経済記事ではこ

ういった表記をする場合がある．「～パーセント」と訳すことが多い．"more than A" は「A を超えて，A 超」という意味である．A は含まれないことに注意する．

p.38 ℓ.3	new findings: 新知見	
p.38 ℓ.3-4	did come as a surprise: 驚きだった	
p.38 ℓ.4	Michael Ferrell: マイケル・フェレル	
p.38 ℓ.4	Coalition for the Homeless: ホームレス連合	
p.38 ℓ.5	turnaround: 方向転換	
p.38 ℓ.5	economy: 経済	
p.38 ℓ.6	in the very near future: 近い将来	
p.38 ℓ.6	it's most likely to get worse: 事態はさらに悪くなる可能性がある	
p.38 ℓ.7	Census Bureau:（アメリカ）国勢調査局	
p.38 ℓ.7	median household income: 平均家計収入，平均家計所得，中位世帯収入	
p.38 ℓ.8	median: 中位	
p.38 ℓ.8-9	half earned more and half earned less: 損得どちらも半ば	
p.38 ℓ.9	income: 所得	
p.38 ℓ.11-12	in poverty: 貧困状態で	
p.38 ℓ.12	largest number: より多くの人数	
p.38 ℓ.13	more than one-fourth of : ～の4分の1超	
p.38 ℓ.13	blacks: 黒人	
p.38 ℓ.13	Hispanics: ヒスパニック（スペイン語を話す人々：ヒスパニック，ラテン・アメリカ系アメリカ人，スペイン系アメリカ人）	
p.38 ℓ.14	Hispanic whites: ヒスパニック系の白人	
p.38 ℓ.15	economic measures: 景気対策，経済措置	
p.38 ℓ.15	women in full-time: フルタイムで働く女性	
p.38 ℓ.15	year-round: 一年中の，通年の	
p.39 ℓ.17	without health insurance: 医療保険を持たない	
p.39 ℓ.20	through their employers: 彼らの雇用主を通して	
p.39 ℓ.21	Economic Policy Institute: 経済政策機関	
p.39 ℓ.23	facing fewer barriers: 障害にほとんど直面していない	
p.39 ℓ.23-24	new health care law: 医療保険改革法	
p.39 ℓ.25	Health reform: 医療保険制度改革	
p.39 ℓ.25	played a key role: 重要な役割を演じる	
p.39 ℓ.25	stem: 阻止する	
p.39 ℓ.26	workplace: 職場	
p.39 ℓ.26	coverage for : ～に対する保険適用	

p.39 ℓ.26   young adults: 若い成人
p.39 ℓ.26-27 Patient Protection and Affordable Care Act: 患者保護医療費軽減法
p.39 ℓ.27   commonly: 普通に，通常，一般的に
p.39 ℓ.27   provisions: 条項，規定
p.39 ℓ.28   up to ：～まで
p.39 ℓ.28-29 their parents' employer-sponsored health insurance policies: 両親の雇用主が保証する保険証書
p.39 ℓ.30   driving force: 原動力，駆動力
p.39 ℓ.30   unemployment: 失業（状態）
p.39 ℓ.31-32 look for work: 職を探す
p.39 ℓ.34   housing market crash: 住宅市場の崩壊
p.39 ℓ.35   construction worker: 建設（土木）作業員，建設労働者
p.39 ℓ.35   Richard Scanlon: リチャード・スキャンロン
p.39 ℓ.39   Family Promise: ファミリープロミス
p.39 ℓ.39   national group: 政府系団体
p.39 ℓ.40   Director: 所長
p.39 ℓ.40   Terry Lindemann: テリー・リンデマン
p.39 ℓ.40-41 religious organization: 宗教団体

Reading Comprehension Questions

次の各文が，本文の内容に合っていればTを，合っていない場合はFを，括弧内に記入してください．

1. (　) The American recession lasted from December of 2007 to June of 2009.
2. (　) Michael Ferrell said unless there's a turnaround within the economy in the very near future, the poverty rate is most likely to get worse.
3. (　) The Census Bureau says median household income did not fall more than two percent from 2009 to 2010.
4. (　) The Census Bureau says more than four million people were living in poverty.
5. (　) Women in full-time, year-round jobs continued to earn an average of seventy-seven percent as much as men did.
6. (　) Most Americans who have health insurance do not get it through their employers.
7. (　) The Patient Protection and Affordable Care Act, is commonly known as health reform.

8. (　　) Experts do not say the biggest driving force of poverty is unemployment.
9. (　　) Las Vegas, Nevada, is famous for its casinos and hotels.
10. (　　) Family Promise is a national group that helps people get foods and hotels.

Listening Comprehension Questions

次の英語を聴いて空欄を埋めてください．

〔00:05-00:37〕

This is IN THE NEWS in VOA Special English. A new report says the (　　　　) (　　　) in the United States last year was the (　　　　) since (　　　). The official rate was (　　　) percent, up from 14.3 percent in 2009. Poverty meant yearly (　　　　), or earnings, of less than (　　　　) (　　　　) (　　　) (　　　　) dollars for a family of four.

English Composition

次の日本文を英文に直してください．

1. アメリカの景気後退は 2007 年 12 月から 2009 年 6 月まで続いた．(last を使って)

2. およそ 1,400 万人のアメリカ人が失業状態となっている．(be unemployed を使って)

3. ネバダ州のラスベガスはカジノやホテルで有名な都市である．(be famous for を使って)

ひとくちコラム

　アメリカ経済は 1929 年の大恐慌に次ぐ，長く深い景気後退を経て，2009 年 6 月を底にして回復過程にある．2008 年 9 月のリーマンショック，金融市場の混乱など深刻な経済の落ち込みを経て，オバマ政権の大規模な景気対策や金融安定化策の発動により，2009 年 6 月を境に回復過程に入った．しかし，貧困水準は 2010 年に 1993 年以来最悪となった．貧困にはさまざまな原因がある．最大の原因である失業に対し政府はどう関わるのか．民間部門の活力に期待するのか，政府が介入し対策を立てるのか．アメリカの将来に禍根を残さないためにも，貧困対策は現在のアメリカ社会における大きな課題である．

Unit 9   Education

Children at U.S. School Show Their Support for Victims in Japan

http://learningenglish.voanews.com/a/1977466.html

出典：VOA, Public Domain
http://learningenglish.voanews.com/content/children-us-school-support-japan--118955664/113778.html

〔00:29-03:55〕

1   Some schoolchildren in the United States have been folding cranes. They want to show they care about the victims of the March eleventh earthquake and tsunami in Japan.

   Almost forty Japanese-American students attend Somerville Elementary
5 School in Ridgewood, New Jersey. But all five hundred twenty-five students at the school have heard about the disasters. So they have decorated their school with paper origami cranes. Their wish is for a speedy recovery for the Japanese people.

   Art teacher Samantha Stankiewicz says the activity gives students a way to express empathy for victims.
10 SAMANTHA STANKIEWICZ: "For children, the folding of the cranes has been a really positive way for them to feel like they're actively engaged, even though the cranes are symbolic."

   These students thought out loud as they folded cranes in the school library.
   BOY: "The crane is a symbol of hope, so we try to have a lot of hope for those
15 people in Japan."
   GIRL: "It makes me feel really happy that everyone's caring for another country."

GIRL: "I feel sad for them, like really sad for them. But I also feel happy for us, because we are really trying to help out."

And that help is not just in the form of paper cranes. The school principal, Lorna Oates-Santos, says children at Somerville Elementary have raised about two thousand dollars for disaster relief agencies.

LORNA OATES-SANTOS: "We will be donating that money to the American Red Cross and Save the Children. They are two groups that are ready on the ground in Japan to help the people of Japan."

The school has a television club that produces weekly programs on different subjects. Fourth-grade teacher Gabrielle King is director of the club, and says the students are involved in the school's efforts.

GABRIELLE KING: "When the earthquake happened, the children wanted to know what they could do to inform other students and raise awareness for the people in Japan. So, we decided to do a show on the earthquake, and to also making the cranes, the origami cranes."

Some American children have shown their feelings for the victims in Japan in other ways. Yasuhisa Kawamura is Japan's deputy consul general in New York.

YASUHISA KAWAMURA: "One American young girl dropped by the consulate a couple days ago with her own painting. The painting shows the two countries, Japan and the United States, shaking hands over the ocean, and saying 'We are with you.' So, we are very, very moved and touched by this young girl's expression."

And that's the VOA Special English Education Report. The East Asia Program at Cornell University in the United States has a lesson plan and directions for folding origami cranes. You can find a link at voaspecialenglish.com. I'm Steve Ember.

読解のための語彙，文法および構文

- *p.43 ℓ.1* schoolchildren: 児童
- *p.43 ℓ.1* folding cranes: ツルを（折り紙で）折る
- *p.43 ℓ.2-3* victims of the March eleventh earthquake and tsunami in Japan: 2011年3月11日に起きた東日本大震災と津波による犠牲者
- *p.43 ℓ.4* Japanese-American: 日系アメリカ人
- *p.43 ℓ.4-5* Somerville Elementary School in Ridgewood, New Jersey: ニュージャージー州のリッジウッドにあるサマービル小学校

Unit 9 Children at U.S. School Show Their Support for Victims in Japan *45*

- *p.43 ℓ.5-6* **all five hundred twenty-five students at the school**: 総勢 525 名の小学生
- *p.43 ℓ.7* **paper origami cranes**: 折り鶴
- *p.43 ℓ.7* **recovery**: 立ち直り，復興，再生
- *p.43 ℓ.7* **Japanese people**: 日本国民
- *p.43 ℓ.8* **art teacher**: 美術の教師
- *p.43 ℓ.8* **Samantha Stankiewicz**: サマンサ・スタンクウィッツ
- *p.43 ℓ.8* **activity**: 活動
- *p.43 ℓ.9* **empathy**: 共感，思いやり，感情移入
- *p.43 ℓ.11* **positive way for them to feel like they're actively engaged**: 自分たちが積極的に関わっていると感じることができる方法
- *p.43 ℓ.11* **even though ～**：～であっても
- *p.43 ℓ.12* **symbolic**: 象徴的
- *p.43 ℓ.13* **think out loud**: 独り言をいう．課題文では記者のインタビューに対して自分の意見を表明しているので「自分の考えを述べる」という意味．
- *p.43 ℓ.14* **symbol of hope**: 希望のシンボル
- *p.43 ℓ.16* **care for**: 思いやりを持って考える，大事に思う
- *p.44 ℓ.17* **help out**: 役立つ
- *p.44 ℓ.19* **school principal**: 校長
- *p.44 ℓ.20* **Lorna Oates-Santos**: ローナ・オートサントス
- *p.44 ℓ.20-21* **raised about two thousand dollars for disaster relief agencies**: 災害救助機関に寄付するためにおよそ 2000 ドルの寄付金を集めた
- *p.44 ℓ.22-23* **American Red Cross**：アメリカの赤十字
- *p.44 ℓ.23* **Save the Children**: セーブ・ザ・チルドレン
  【URL】http://www.savethechildren.org/
- *p.44 ℓ.23-24* **on the ground**: 現場で
- *p.44 ℓ.25* **television club**: 放送部
- *p.44 ℓ.25* **produce weekly programs**: 週間番組を制作する
- *p.44 ℓ.26* **Fourth-grade**: 4 年生
- *p.44 ℓ.26* **Gabrielle King**: ガブリエル・キング
- *p.44 ℓ.26-27* **the students are involved in the school's efforts**: 児童たちは小学校の活動に参加している
- *p.44 ℓ.32-33* **in other ways**: 他の方法で
- *p.44 ℓ.33* **Yasuhisa Kawamura**: 川村泰久
- *p.44 ℓ.33* **Japan's deputy consul general**: 日本総領事館副領事
- *p.44 ℓ.34* **drop by**: 立ち寄る

p.44 ℓ.34   consulate: 領事館

p.44 ℓ.35   a couple days ago: 2日前に

p.44 ℓ.38   expression: 表現（法）

p.44 ℓ.39   Education Report: 教育レポート

p.44 ℓ.39-40   The East Asia Program at Cornell University: コーネル大学の東アジアプログラム

p.44 ℓ.40-41   a lesson plan and directions for folding origami cranes: 折り鶴の授業計画と指導案

Reading Comprehension Questions

次の各文が，本文の内容に合っていればTを，合っていない場合はFを，括弧内に記入してください．

1. (　) Some schoolchildren in the United States have been folding cranes.
2. (　) Almost sixty Japanese-American students attend Somerville Elementary School in Ridgewood,
3. (　) A few students at the school have heard about the disasters.
4. (　) Art teacher Samantha Stankiewicz says the activity gives students a way to express empathy for victims.
5. (　) The folding of the cranes has not been any positive way for them to feel like they're actively engaged.
6. (　) Children at Somerville Elementary have raised about two thousand dollars for disaster relief agencies.
7. (　) The school has a radio club that produces weekly programs on different subjects.
8. (　) Many American children have shown their feelings for the victims in Japan in other ways.
9. (　) One American young girl dropped by the consulate a couple days ago with her own painting.
10. (　) Yasuhisa Kawamura is Japan's deputy consul general in New York was very moved and touched by this young girl's expression.

Unit 9 Children at U.S. School Show Their Support for Victims in Japan 47

Listening Comprehension Questions

次の英語を聴いて空欄を埋めてください．

http://learningenglish.voanews.com/audio/audio/6473.html

[00:00-00:28]

This is the VOA Special English Education Report. (　　　) are large birds with long legs and necks. In Japan and other East Asian cultures, they (　　　) (　　　) and (　　　) (　　　). Japanese (　　　) says a person who (　　　) one (　　　) paper cranes (　　　) the right to (　　　) a wish.

English Composition

次の日本文を英文に直してください．

1. アメリカにはツルを折り続けている小学生もいる．(some と have been folding を使って)

　_____

2. 私たちはそのお金をアメリカ赤十字に寄付する予定です．(donate を使って)

　_____

3. 一人の幼い少女が 2 日前に総領事館に立ち寄った．(drop by を使って)

　_____

ひとくちコラム

2011 年 3 月 11 日に発生した東日本大震災の被災者，被災地域に対し国内だけではなく，海外からも多くの支援があった．外務省によると，日本は当時，在日米軍による支援を正式に要請した．在日米軍司令部によると，米軍は最大時には人員約 2 万 4,500 名，艦船 24 隻，航空機 189 機を投入して「トモダチ作戦」と称し，大規模な救援活動を実施した．また食料品等約 280 トン，水約 770 万リットル，燃料約 4.5 万リットルを配給した．こうした政府関連の支援だけではなく，課題文のようなアメリカの小学生による心のケアも含め，民間からも多くの支援やボランティア活動があったことを忘れてはならない．

Unit 10

Healthcare

Have a headache? You are not alone

http://learningenglish.voanews.com/a/2259131.html

出典：VOA, Public Domain
http://gdb.voanews.com/85BB2592-B816-4353-BD38-F1499B4B73C5_w640_r1_s.jpg

00:49-05:36

1   The National Headache Foundation says more than 45 million people in the United States suffer chronic headaches. Such a headache causes severe pain that goes away but returns later. Some headaches may prove difficult and require time to treat. But many experts today are working toward cures or major help for chronic headaches.

   The U.S. Headache Consortium is a group with seven member organizations. They are working to improve treatment of one kind of headache -- the migraine. Some people experience this kind of pain as often as two weeks every month. The National Headache Foundation says about 70 percent of migraine sufferers are women.

   Some people describe the pain as throbbing, causing pressure in the head. Others compare it to someone driving a sharp object into the head. Migraine headaches cause Americans to miss at least 150 million workdays each year.

A migraine can be mild. But it also can be so severe that a person cannot live a normal life.

One migraine sufferer is Curtis Croley of Ellicott City in Maryland. He had head pain as a child. Mr. Croley says he does not know what kind of headaches they were. But when he suffered severe headaches as an adult, doctors identified the problem as migraine.

Today, Mr. Croley produces and directs films and videos. He says months can pass without a headache. But then he will have three migraines within a month. If he takes the medicine his doctor ordered early in his headache, it controls the pain in his head. If not, the pain becomes extremely bad. Sometimes he has had to be treated with a combination of drugs in a hospital.

Some people take medicine every day to prevent or ease migraine headaches. Others use medicine to control pain already developed. Doctors treating migraine sufferers often order medicines from a group of drugs known as triptans.

Most migraines react at least partly to existing medicine. And most people can use existing medicine without experiencing bad effects. Doctors sometimes use caffeine to treat migraine headaches. Interestingly, caffeine can also cause some migraines.

Medical experts have long recognized the work of the Mayo Clinic in Rochester, Minnesota. The Mayo Clinic says several foods are suspected of being "triggers" that start migraines. They include cheese and alcoholic drinks. Food additives like salt and monosodium glutamate also may be triggers.

The Mayo Clinic tells patients to avoid strong smells that have seemingly started migraines in the past. Some people react badly to products like perfume, even if they have a pleasant smell.

The clinic's experts say aerobic exercise can help migraine sufferers. Aerobic exercise increases a person's heart rate. It can include walking, swimming or riding a bicycle. But a sudden start to hard exercise can cause headaches. So it is a good idea to perform some mild exercises before beginning activities that require more energy.

読解のための語彙，文法および構文

p.48 ℓ.2	headache(s): 頭痛
p.48 ℓ.1	National Headache Foundation:（アメリカ）頭痛財団
	【URL】http://www.headaches.org/
p.48 ℓ.1	more than 45 million: 4,500万人を超える
p.48 ℓ.2	suffer:（肉体的・精神的に）苦しむ，（痛みなどに）苦しむ
p.48 ℓ.2	chronic headaches: 慢性頭痛
p.48 ℓ.3	goes away but returns later:（痛みが）なくなっても，後からぶりかえす
p.48 ℓ.3	prove: 〜とわかる
p.48 ℓ.3	difficult: 治りづらい
p.48 ℓ.3-4	require time to treat: 治療するのに時間が必要になる
p.48 ℓ.4-5	working toward cures or major help for chronic headaches: 慢性頭痛の軽減に取り組んでいる
p.48 ℓ.6	The U.S. Headache Consortium: アメリカ頭痛コンソーシアム
p.48 ℓ.7	kind of: いわば
p.48 ℓ.7	migraine: 偏頭痛
p.48 ℓ.8	as often as two weeks every month: 毎月2週間ほどの頻度で
p.48 ℓ.9	migraine sufferers: 偏頭痛に悩む人々
p.48 ℓ.11	pain as throbbing: 拍動性の痛みとして
p.48 ℓ.12	compare A to B: AをBに例える
p.48 ℓ.12	drive:「強打する，突進する」の意味がある．"driving a sharp object into the head" は鋭い物を頭に差し込むような感じを表現するために使われている．
p.48 ℓ.13	150 million workdays: 1億5,000万日
p.49 ℓ.15	normal life: 通常の生活
p.49 ℓ.16	Curtis Croley: カーチス・クローリー
p.49 ℓ.16	Ellicott City: エリコットシティ
p.49 ℓ.16	Maryland: メリーランド州
p.49 ℓ.18	identified: 特定する
p.49 ℓ.20	produces and directs films and videos: 映画やビデオを制作し，監督する
p.49 ℓ.21	pass without a headache: 頭痛なく過ごす
p.49 ℓ.22, 25	take medicine: 薬を飲む
p.49 ℓ.22	order: 指示する
p.49 ℓ.23	If not: そうしないと
p.49 ℓ.23	becomes extremely bad: ひどくなる
p.49 ℓ.24	combination of drugs in a hospital: 病院で複数の薬を併用する

p.49 ℓ.26	pain already developed:	すでに発現している痛み
p.49 ℓ.27	order medicines:	薬品を注文する
p.49 ℓ.27	a group of drugs:	薬物群
p.49 ℓ.27	triptans:	トリプタン（片頭痛の特効薬）
p.49 ℓ.28	react:	効き目がある
p.49 ℓ.28	existing medicine:	現在ある薬
p.49 ℓ.29	without experiencing bad effects:	副作用なく
p.49 ℓ.30	caffeine:	カフェイン
p.49 ℓ.32	medical experts:	医療専門家
p.49 ℓ.32	Mayo Clinic:	メイヨ・クリニック【URL】http://www.mayoclinic.org/
p.49 ℓ.33	Rochester:	ロチェスター
p.49 ℓ.33	Minnesota:	ミネソタ州
p.49 ℓ.34	triggers:	引き金
p.49 ℓ.34-35	food additives:	食品添加物
p.49 ℓ.35	monosodium glutamate:	グルタミン酸ナトリウム（MSG）．アメリカではMSGと呼ばれる．化学調味料で主に中華料理店で使われている．アレルギーを起こす人がいるため，店頭に"NO MSG"と看板を掲げている店も多い．
p.49 ℓ.36	strong smells:	臭いのきつい
p.49 ℓ.36	seemingly:	～のように見える，一見したところ
p.49 ℓ.37	perfume:	香水
p.49 ℓ.38	pleasant smell:	心地よい香り
p.49 ℓ.39	aerobic exercise:	有酸素運動
p.49 ℓ.40	heart rate:	心拍（数）
p.49 ℓ.41	hard exercise:	激しい運動

Reading Comprehension Questions

次の各文が，本文の内容に合っていればTを，合っていない場合はFを，括弧内に記入してください．

1. (　　) More than 45 million people in the United States suffer chronic headaches
2. (　　) The U.S. Headache Consortium is a group with six member organizations.
3. (　　) Some people describe the pain as throbbing, causing pressure in the head.

52

4. (　　) Mr. Croley says he knows what kind of headaches they were.
5. (　　) Sometimes Mr. Croley has had to be treated with a combination of drugs in a hospital.
6. (　　) Some people take medicine every day to prevent or ease migraine headaches.
7. (　　) Most migraines do not react at least partly to existing medicine.
8. (　　) The Mayo Clinic says several foods are not suspected of being "triggers" that start migraines.
9. (　　) The Mayo Clinic tells patients not to avoid strong smells that would cause migraines.
10. (　　) The clinic's experts say aerobic exercise can help migraine sufferers.

Listening Comprehension Questions

次の英語を聴いて空欄を埋めてください．

http://learningenglish.voanews.com/audio/audio/358326.html

00:02-00:48

From VOA Learning English, this is Science in the News. I'm Steve Ember. Today Barbara Klein and I tell about (　　　　), the (　　　) that (　　　　　) almost everyone at some time.

Have you (　　　) a headache recently? If your (　　　　) is yes, you are like many millions of people worldwide who (　　　　　) pain in the head. The pain can be (　　　　), mild and (　　　) by a simple (　　　　　) like aspirin. Or, it can be (　　　　).

English Composition

次の日本文を英文に直してください．

1. 米国頭痛財団によると 4,500 万人を超える人々が慢性頭痛に苦しんでいる．(suffer を使って)

2. 医師らは偏頭痛の治療にカフェインを使うこともある．(use を使って)

3. しかし，いきなり激しい運動を行うと頭痛の原因になることがある．(caus を使って)

ひとくちコラム

『NEDO 海外レポート』によると，アメリカ人の8人に1人が慢性偏頭痛に苦しんでいる．慢性偏頭痛が起きると晴天で気持ちの良い日でも自宅にこもり，痛みを和らげるためにおとなしくしていなければならない．市販の鎮痛剤の使用を繰り返すことで副作用の懸念もある．偏頭痛に対処するため，課題のように官民でさまざまな対策や治療法が開発されている．日本でも偏頭痛については，日本頭痛学会，日本神経学会をはじめとしてさまざまな研究が行われている．

Unit 11 Public Welfare

People with Disabilities Achieve New Opportunities

http://learningenglish.voanews.com/a/2235108.html

出典：U.S. National Library of Medicine, Public Domain
http://ihm.nlm.nih.gov/luna/servlet/detail/NLMNLM~1~1~101453799~197836:While-convalescing-you-can-study-Ja?sort=Title%2CSubject_MeSH_Term%2CCreator_Person%2CCreator_Organization&qvq=q:wheel+chair;sort:Title,Subject_MeSH_Term,Creator_Person,Creator_Organization;lc:NLMNLM~1~1&mi=3&trs=6

00:26-04:29

1　　A government report says more people with disabilities work as janitors or building cleaners than any other job. People with physical or mental disabilities are less likely to be employed than people without a disability. And those who are employed are more likely to work in lower paying jobs, and to earn less than their
5　co-workers with no disability.

　　Meg Grigal works with an organization called Think College. That group helps colleges and universities provide courses, social opportunities and job training for people with mental disabilities. Many of the students have Down's syndrome. Ms. Grigal says the students gain from higher education just like anyone else hoping
10　to earn more in future employment by going to college.

　　"I think we are starting to be able to document the economic impact for people with intellectual disabilities that having them go to college even if it's not for a degree is going to improve their employment outcome." Ms. Grigal says the most common reason students with intellectual disabilities do not go to college is because their teachers and parents do not think they can do it.

"You can only believe in what you have seen is possible. And if in your entire career or your entire child's life, you've been told people with intellectual disabilities can't go to college, then that is your knee-jerk reaction when you are broached with an opportunity."

There is a campaign to encourage young people with mental disabilities to consider college. These students are part of that campaign. "College is kind of like a challenge. You get to learn new things that you are not learning in high school."

"The reason I am going to college is to get an education and for everybody to know who I am. I want my family to be proud I want my friends to be proud."

One opportunity is at Virginia Commonwealth University. Students with mental disabilities receive a special certificate after they take classes for 30 months at VCU. Liz Getzel is the director of postsecondary initiatives at the university.

She says VCU discovered one student who had no idea how artistic he was. "He had never been exposed to that. He drew a self-portrait of himself that looked like a photograph. We are finding this more and more. This opens them up in terms of the amazing amount of talent they have." Talent to get a good job and be an active member of the community.

Congress passed the Americans with Disabilities Act, known as the ADA, more than 20 years ago. The law made it easier for people with disabilities to get jobs and use public transportation and public buildings.

読解のための語彙，文法および構文

- *p.54 ℓ.1* government report: 政府報告書（USGR）
- *p.54 ℓ.1* people with disabilities: 障害を持つ人々，障害者
- *p.54 ℓ.1* janitors: 用務員，清掃作業員
- *p.54 ℓ.2* building cleaners: ビルの掃除人
- *p.54 ℓ.2* people with physical or mental disabilities: 身体障害，精神障害を持つ人々
- *p.54 ℓ.3* less likely to be employed: 雇用される機会が少ない
- *p.54 ℓ.3* people without a disability: 障害がない人々，健常者
- *p.54 ℓ.4* lower paying jobs: 賃金の低い仕事
- *p.54 ℓ.5* co-workers: 仕事仲間
- *p.54 ℓ.6* Meg Grigal: メグ・グリゴル
- *p.54 ℓ.6* Think College: シンクカレッジ
- *p.54 ℓ.6-7* helps colleges and universities provide: 単科大学や総合大学が〜を提供するの

を支援する

- *p.54 ℓ.7* social opportunities: 社会的機会
- *p.54 ℓ.7* job training: 職業訓練
- *p.54 ℓ.8* Down's syndrome: ダウン症，ダウン症候群
- *p.54 ℓ.9* higher education: 高等教育
- *p.54 ℓ.11* document: 実証する
- *p.54 ℓ.11* economic impact: 経済的影響
- *p.54 ℓ.12* intellectual disabilities: 知的障害
- *p.54 ℓ.13* degree: 学位
- *p.54 ℓ.13* employment outcome: 雇用効果
- *p.54 ℓ.14* common reason: 共通の理由
- *p.55 ℓ.16* You can only believe ：インタビューで話をしている点に注意する．「実際に見たら，（知的障害を負っていても大学に通うことが）可能であると信じられる」と言っている．
- *p.55 ℓ.16* what you have seen: 実際に見てきたこと
- *p.55 ℓ.18* knee-jerk: 型にはまった
- *p.55 ℓ.18* reaction: 反応
- *p.55 ℓ.18* then that is your kee-jerk reaction: 話者は「（人から話を聞いて先入観があるから）型にはまった反応しかできない」と言いたいのである．
- *p.55 ℓ.18-19* you are broached with ：〜について提案を受ける，〜に関する話を切り出される．
- *p.55 ℓ.20* encourage: 奨励する
- *p.55 ℓ.21* consider college: 大学進学を考える
- *p.55 ℓ.22* challenge: 挑戦
- *p.55 ℓ.22* get to ：〜を始める，〜に取り掛かる
- *p.55 ℓ.23* get an education: 教育を受ける
- *p.55 ℓ.25* Virginia Commonwealth University: バージニアコモンウェルス大学（VCU）
- *p.55 ℓ.26* special certificate: 特別修了証
- *p.55 ℓ.27* Liz Getzel: リズ・ゲッゼル
- *p.55 ℓ.27* director: 責任者
- *p.55 ℓ.27* postsecondary initiatives: 中等教育後の指導
- *p.55 ℓ.28* artistic: 芸術的な
- *p.55 ℓ.29* exposed to ：〜に触れる
- *p.55 ℓ.29* drew a self-portrait: 自画像を描く
- *p.55 ℓ.30* photograph: 写真

Unit 11 People with Disabilities Achieve New Opportunities 57

p.55 ℓ.30 in terms of　:～の点から見て

p.55 ℓ.31 talent: 才能，素質

p.55 ℓ.33 Congress: 議会

p.55 ℓ.33 pass: 可決する

p.55 ℓ.33 Americans with Disabilities Act: アメリカ障害者法，障害を持つアメリカ人法（ADA）

p.55 ℓ.35 public transportation and public buildings: 公共交通や公共施設

Reading Comprehension Questions

次の各文が，本文の内容に合っていればTを，合っていない場合はFを，括弧内に記入してください．

1. (　) A government report says more people with disabilities work as janitors or building cleaners than any other job.
2. (　) People with physical or mental disabilities are less likely to be employed than people without a disability.
3. (　) Meg Grigal doesn't work with an organization called Think College.
4. (　) Ms. Grigal says the students do not gain from higher education.
5. (　) Ms. Grigal says the most common reason students with intellectual disabilities do not go to college is because their teachers and parents do not think they can do it.
6. (　) There is not a campaign to encourage young people with mental disabilities to consider college. T
7. (　) Students with mental disabilities receive a special certificate after they take classes for 30 months at VCU.
8. (　) Liz Getzel is the student of postsecondary initiatives at the university.
9. (　) VCU did not discover one student who had no idea how artistic he was.
10. (　) Congress passed the Americans with Disabilities Act, known as the ADA, more than 20 years ago.

Listening Comprehension Questions

次の英語を聴いて空欄を埋めてください．

http://learningenglish.voanews.com/audio/audio/269135.html

00:05-00:24

From VOA Learning English, welcome to (　　　) Is (　　　　) in Special English. I'm Kelly Jean Kelly. And I'm Jim Tedder. Today we (　　　) (　　) what's (　　　　) (　　　) (　　　　), (　　　　) and (　　　　) for people with (　　　　　).

English Composition

次の日本文を英文に直してください．

1. メグ・グリゴル氏は「シンク・カレッジ」と呼ばれる組織と連携をとっている．（work with を使って）

2. 精神障害を持つ若者の大学進学を奨励するキャンペーンがある．（encourage を使って）

3. VCU は，自分がどんなに芸術性があるかを知らなかった一人の学生を見いだした．（discover を使って）

ひとくちコラム

アメリカでは障害を持つ人々の雇用，公的サービス（公共交通機関），民間の施設やサービス，救済措置などが規定された「アメリカ障害者法（ADA）」が1990年に施行された．日本でも障害を持つ人々の自立および社会参加の支援等の基本的理念を定め，国，地方公共団体等の責務を明らかにした「障害者基本法」が1970年に制定された．ADAは，障害者の雇用，公共機関の利用，使用する言語，聴覚障害者の電話利用，手話通訳者の手配など，あらゆる分野において障害者に対する差別を禁じ，障害者の機会平等を保障している．

Unit 12　　Law

U.S. Supreme Court Upholds Health Care Law, Strikes Down Much of Immigration Law

http://learningenglish.voanews.com/a/2124256.html

アメリカ最高裁判所
出典：Wikimedia Commons, Public Domain
http://commons.wikimedia.org/wiki/File:
US_Supreme_Court_-_original.jpg?uselang=ja

00:39-04:30

1　　In early twenty-ten, Congress approved -- and President Obama signed into law -- The Patient Protection and Affordable Care Act. The law came to be known as "Obamacare." It is the most important legislative priority of the Obama administration. The law was written to help Americans with rising health care costs and the often serious financial problems many Americans have with health care.

　　In the law is what is called an "individual mandate." And, this mandate requires every American citizen to have health insurance by twenty-fourteen or face a financial penalty.

　　Among the law's supporters are those who believe health care is a right, not a privilege. But many are opposed to the law. In fact, twenty-six states sued to overturn it. They said the Constitution does not permit Congress to force people to buy a product they may neither want nor need.

　　But, public opinion studies show some parts of the law are very popular with

Americans. They include requiring insurance companies to pay for preventative health care and banning limits on the amount of money insurance companies pay for care.

Also popular is a ban on denying insurance for people who already have health problems. This is usually called a preexisting condition. The law also permits people to be covered by their parent's insurance until age twenty-six.

Many people on both sides of the debate were surprised when the Court upheld the law, by a vote of five to four. The decision was a major victory for the president. In the majority was Chief Justice John Roberts, a conservative who was believed to be against the individual mandate. But he joined with liberals on the Court in calling the mandate a tax. He said the Constitution and the Court's own rulings have established that Congress has the power to impose a tax.

President Obama called the ruling a victory for Americans who cannot afford health care.

PRESIDENT OBAMA: "I know there will be a lot of discussion today about the politics of all this, about who won and who lost, that's how these things tend to be viewed here in Washington. But that discussion completely misses the point. Whatever the politics, today's decision was a victory for people all over this country whose lives will be more secure because of this law and the Supreme Court's decision to uphold it."

Some parts of the law go into effect before the presidential election this November. Mr. Obama's expected challenger in the twenty-twelve election -- Republican Mitt Romney -- was disappointed with the ruling.

If Republicans keep control of the House and gain control of the Senate, and if Mr. Romney wins this November's election, the law could be cancelled next year.

読解のための語彙，文法および構文

タイトル U.S. Supreme Court: アメリカ最高裁判所

タイトル p.60 ℓ.34 uphold: 支持する

タイトル Health Care Law: 正確には Patient Protection and Affordable Care Act.「オバマケア」と呼ばれる医療改革法のこと．

タイトル Strikes Down: 無効にする

タイトル Immigration Law: 移民法

p.59 ℓ.1 early twenty-ten: 2010 年初頭

p.59 ℓ.1 Congress approve: 議会は承認する

Unit 12 U.S. Supreme Court Upholds Health Care Law, Strikes Down Much of Immigration Law

p.59 ℓ.2	Patient Protection and Affordable Care Act: 医療保険制度改革法は「Obamacare」（オバマケア）と呼ばれている．
p.59 ℓ.3	the most important legislative priority: 優先させるべき最重要法案
p.59 ℓ.3-4	Obama administration: オバマ政権
p.59 ℓ.4-5	rising health care costs: 増大する医療費
p.59 ℓ.5-6	serious financial problems many Americans have with health care: 多くのアメリカ人が医療を受ける際に陥る深刻な金銭問題
p.59 ℓ.7	individual mandate: 個人強制保険
p.59 ℓ.8	American citizen: アメリカ国民
p.59 ℓ.8	health insurance: 健康保険
p.59 ℓ.8	by twenty-fourteen: 2014年までに
p.59 ℓ.9	financial penalty: 罰金
p.59 ℓ.10	law's supporters: 法案の支持者
p.59 ℓ.10-11	not a privilege: 特権ではない
p.59 ℓ.11	be opposed to～：～に反対している
p.59 ℓ.11	in fact: 実際
p.59 ℓ.11	sue: 訴訟を起こす
p.59 ℓ.12	overturn: 覆す
p.59 ℓ.12	Constitution: 憲法
p.59 ℓ.12	Congress: 議会
p.59 ℓ.12	force people to　：人々に～することを強制する
p.59 ℓ.14	public opinion: 世論
p.60 ℓ.15	insurance companies: 保険会社
p.60 ℓ.15-16	pay for preventative health care: 予防医療についても支払う
p.60 ℓ.16	banning limits on　：～に制限をかけることを禁じる
p.60 ℓ.18	ban on denying insurance for　：～が保険に加入するのを拒絶することを禁じる
p.60 ℓ.18-19	health problems: 健康上の問題
p.60 ℓ.19	preexisting condition: 契約前発病，既存欠陥（契約前にすでに被保険者が持っていた健康上の欠陥）．アメリカでは契約前の既存欠陥が原因となる高度障害に関しては加入後の一定期間は免責にしている．
p.60 ℓ.20	cover: 保険で保証する
p.60 ℓ.21	debate: 議論
p.60 ℓ.22	vote of five to four: 5対4の投票
p.60 ℓ.22	major victory: 大きな勝利

- p.60 ℓ.23　majority: 大多数，過半数
- p.60 ℓ.23　Chief Justice: 最高裁判所長官
- p.60 ℓ.23　John Roberts: ジョン・ロバーツ
- p.60 ℓ.23　conservative: 保守派，保守党（この記事が書かれた2012年7月は保守政党は民主党）
- p.60 ℓ.25　tax: 精勤
- p.60 ℓ.25-26　Court's own rulings: 最高裁の決定
- p.60 ℓ.26　impose a tax: 課税する
- p.60 ℓ.29　a lot of discussion: 多くの議論
- p.60 ℓ.30　politics: 政治
- p.60 ℓ.30　who won and who lost: だれかが勝ってだれかが負けた
- p.60 ℓ.30-31　tend to be viewed: 〜と見られる傾向がある
- p.60 ℓ.31-32　miss the point: ピントがずれている
- p.60 ℓ.32　whatever: なんであろうとも
- p.60 ℓ.35　go into effect: 発効する，実施する
- p.60 ℓ.36　Mr. Obama's expected challenger in the twenty-twelve election: この記事は2012年7月9日に書かれた記事．大統領選は2012年11月6日に行われた．対立候補は共和党のミット・ロムニー氏．

Reading Comprehension Questions

次の各文が，本文の内容に合っていればTを，合っていない場合はFを，括弧内に記入してください．

1. (　) In early twenty-ten, Congress approved the Patient Protection and Affordable Care Act.
2. (　) Obamacare is not the most important legislative priority of the Obama administration.
3. (　) In the law is what is called an "individual mandate."
4. (　) Among the law's supporters are those who believe health care is a right, not a privilege.
5. (　) Public opinion studies do not show some parts of the law are very popular.
6. (　) Also popular is a ban on accepting insurance for people who already have health problems.
7. (　) The decision was a major victory for the president.

Unit 12 U.S. Supreme Court Upholds Health Care Law, Strikes Down Much of Immigration Law   63

8. (　) Many people on both sides of the debate were surprised when the Court upheld the law.
9. (　) President Obama did not call the ruling a victory for Americans who cannot afford health care.
10. (　) President Obama did not know there would be a lot of discussion today about the politics

Listening Comprehension Questions

次の英語を聴いて空欄を埋めてください.

http://learningenglish.voanews.com/audio/audio/157252.html

(00:03-00:32)

Welcome to THIS IS AMERICA in VOA Special English. I'm Christopher Cruise.
Today, we will (　) (　) the recent United States (　) (　) rulings that (　) President Obama's health care law and (　) parts of Arizona's immigration law. We also (　) on a case that (　) (　) the (　) of murderers under the age of eighteen.

English Composition

次の日本文を英文に直してください.

1. その法律は「オバマケア」として知られるようになった.（come to be known as を使って）

   _____

2. しかし多くがその法律に反対している.（oppose to を使って）

   _____

3. ロムニー氏が11月の選挙に勝つと，法律は翌年に無効となる.（win と cancel を使って）

   _____

> **ひとくちコラム**
>
> 　課題文は第2期オバマ政権発足前の話題で終わっているが，2012年11月に行われた大統領選では，オバマ氏が再選した．アメリカの最高裁判所の正面玄関の上部に「法の下における平等な正義（Equal Justice Under Law）」という文字が刻まれている．無保険で医療を受けられない人々の救済を行うためにオバマ氏は医療保険法の改革に着手した．医療保険法の改革は1940年代にトルーマン政権，1990年代にクリントン政権が失敗に終わっている．アメリカには，建国の精神から大きな政権に対し警戒する伝統がある．オバマ政権はその伝統に抗ってでも医療保険法の改革に挑んだのである．
>
> 参考文献：西山隆行「アメリカではなぜ国民皆保険が実現しないのか？：革新主義時代から第二次世界大戦期までの医療保険政策をめぐる政治」『甲南法学』（甲南大学法学会，2008年）
> 　　　　　杉田米行編『日米の医療―制度と倫理』（大阪大学出版会，2008年）
> 　　　　　Yamagishi, Takakazu. *War and Health Insurance Policy in Japan and the United States: World War II to Postwar Reconstruction.* Baltimore: Johns Hopkins University Press, 2011.

Unit 13　　The Making of a Nation

Christmas in 19th Century America

http://learningenglish.voanews.com/a/2321575.html

出典 :VOA, Public Domain
http://gdb.voanews.com/92782FF3-B93C-446A-A062-E2E0FFD13C77_w640_r1_s.jpg

[00:43-05:52]

1　　During this period, Christmas was a very different kind of holiday than it is today. There was no set way of celebrating the day, which was not yet an official holiday. Communities around the country honored the day in different ways. Some observed Christmas as an important Christian religious day honoring the
5　birth of Jesus. Others celebrated the day with parties, music, drinking and eating. And, some communities did not celebrate the day at all.

　　But, it was during this period that Americans began to reinvent the holiday by combining ancient Christmas traditions from different cultures with modern American influences. You can think about the historical people we have been
10 talking about, Andrew Jackson, Martin van Buren and others, and the ways they too might have celebrated Christmas.

　　In 1819, the popular American writer Washington Irving wrote a series of five essays published in a book called "The Sketchbook of Geoffrey Crayon, Gent."

　　The essays describe a wealthy British landowner who invites his farm workers
15 into his home to celebrate Christmas. The landowner recreates a traditional Christmas as it would have been celebrated in the distant past. Irving praised this

looking back to ancient traditions. He liked the idea of different levels of society coming together to enjoy a festive and peaceful holiday. Washington Irving seemed to express concern about the lack of such unifying Christmas traditions in modern America.

Penne Restad wrote a book "Christmas in America: A History." It shows how Americans began to slowly shape Christmas into a unifying national holiday during the first half of the 19th century. She describes how Christmas had different meanings for Americans who came from different cultural and religious backgrounds. Many immigrants brought Christmas traditions from their own countries.

Religion played a big role in how an American might celebrate the holiday. Calvinist Christians banned the celebration of Christmas. But groups such as Episcopalians and Moravians honored the day with religious services and seasonal decorations.

By mid-century, Christian groups began to ignore their religious differences over the meaning of Christmas and honored the day in special ways.

Christmas became an important time for families to celebrate at home. More and more Christian Americans also began to follow the European traditions of Christmas trees and giving gifts. Christians believed that the tree represented Jesus and was also a sign of new beginnings. German immigrants brought their tradition of putting lights, sweets and toys on the branches of evergreen trees placed in their homes.

This tradition of setting up a Christmas tree soon spread to many American homes. So did the practice of giving people presents. As these traditions increased in popularity, the modern trade and business linked to Christmas also grew.

As Christmas became more popular, some states declared the day a state holiday. Louisiana was the first state to make the move in 1837. By 1860, 14 other states had followed. It was not until 1870 that President Ulysses Grant made Christmas a federal holiday.

Unit 13　Christmas in 19th Century America　67

読解のための語彙，文法および構文

p.65 ℓ.1　During this period: テキストにはないが，リスニング課題のナレーションの箇所に 19 世紀前半のアメリカにおけるクリスマスの伝統を取り上げることを言っている．"this period" は 19 世紀前半の時期のこと．

p.65 ℓ.1　Christmas: クリスマス，キリスト降誕祭．不可算名詞である．形容詞を伴う時には a ×××（形容詞）Christmas と表記する．12 月 25 日が当日．復活祭（Easter）とともにキリスト教の最大の行事である．

p.65 ℓ.2　set way: 決まったやり方

p.65 ℓ.2-3　official holiday: 法定休日

p.65 ℓ.3　honor: 称える

p.65 ℓ.4　observe　: ～と見る

p.65 ℓ.4　religious day: 宗教的な日

p.65 ℓ.5　birth of Jesus: イエス・キリストの誕生

p.65 ℓ.5　celebrate: 祝う

p.65 ℓ.6　community: コミュニティー，共同体，地域社会

p.65 ℓ.7　reinvent: 新たに考案する

p.65 ℓ.8-9　combining ancient Christmas traditions from different cultures with modern American influences: 他文化の古いクリスマスの伝統を現代アメリカの影響力と結びつける

p.65 ℓ.9　historical people: 歴史上の人物

p.65 ℓ.10　Andrew Jackson: アンドリュー・ジャクソン（1765 ～ 1845 年）アメリカ第 7 代大統領（1829 ～ 1837 年）

p.65 ℓ.10　Martin van Buren: マーティン・ヴァン・ビューレン（1782 ～ 1862 年）アメリカ第 8 代大統領（1837 ～ 1841 年）

p.65 ℓ.12　Washington Irving: ワシントン・アービング（1783 ～ 1859 年）．アメリカの作家．短編集で知られる．

p.65 ℓ.12-13　wrote a series of five essays published in a book called "The Sketchbook of Geoffrey Crayon, Gent.": 『スケッチ・ブック』という本で出版された 5 つの短編小説を書いた．"The Sketchbook of Geoffrey Crayon, Gent" の邦題は『スケッチ・ブック』である．

p.65 ℓ.14　wealthy: 裕福な

p.65 ℓ.14　landowner: 地主

p.65 ℓ.14　his farm workers: 彼の農場で働いている労働者たち，小作人

p.65 ℓ.15　recreate: 再現する

p.65 ℓ.15-16　traditional Christmas: 伝統的なクリスマス

p.65 ℓ.16	distant past:	はるか昔
p.65 ℓ.16	praise:	称賛する
p.66 ℓ.17	looking back:	過去を振り返る
p.66 ℓ.17	levels of society:	社会水準
p.66 ℓ.18	come together:	協力する
p.66 ℓ.18	festive and peaceful holiday:	陽気で平和な休日
p.66 ℓ.19	concern about :	〜の心配
p.66 ℓ.19	unifying:	求心力のある
p.66 ℓ.21	Penne Restad:	ペン・レスタッド
p.66 ℓ.21	Christmas in America: A History:	『アメリカのクリスマス：歴史』
p.66 ℓ.22	shape:	形作る
p.66 ℓ.23	the first half of the 19th century:	19世紀前半
p.66 ℓ.24-25	religious backgrounds:	宗教的背景
p.66 ℓ.25	immigrant (s):	移民
p.66 ℓ.27	play a big role in :	〜において大きな役割を果たす
p.66 ℓ.28	Calvinist Christians:	カルビン派のクリスチャン
p.66 ℓ.29	Episcopalians:	アメリカ聖公会のクリスチャン
p.66 ℓ.29	Moravians:	モラビア派のクリスチャン
p.66 ℓ.29	religious service:	礼拝
p.66 ℓ.31	by mid-century:	世紀半ばまでに
p.66 ℓ.33	at home:	家庭で
p.66 ℓ.34	European tradition:	ヨーロッパの伝統
p.66 ℓ.35	represent :	〜を象徴する
p.66 ℓ.37	putting lights, sweets and toys on the branches of evergreen trees:	常緑樹の枝にライトやお菓子，おもちゃを置く
p.66 ℓ.39	spread to :	〜に広がる
p.66 ℓ.40-41	increased in popularity:	人気が出た
p.66 ℓ.42	declared :	〜と宣言する
p.66 ℓ.43	Louisiana:	ルイジアナ州
p.66 ℓ.44	follow:	追随する，ならう
p.66 ℓ.44	It was not until 1870 that :	「1870年まで〜しなかった」という意味だが，「1870年になってやっと〜した」と訳すことができる．
p.66 ℓ.44	Ulysses Grant（＝Ulysses Simpson Grant）:	ユリシーズ・シンプソン・グラント（1822〜1885年），アメリカ第18代大統領（1869〜1877年）

Unit 13 Christmas in 19th Century America 69

Reading Comprehension Questions

次の各文が，本文の内容に合っていればTを，合っていない場合はFを，括弧内に記入してください．

1. (   ) During this period, Christmas was a very different kind of holiday than it is today.
2. (   ) Americans did not begin to reinvent the holiday by combining ancient Christmas traditions from different cultures with modern American influences.
3. (   ) In 1800, the popular American writer Washington Irving wrote a series of five essays.
4. (   ) Washington Irving seemed to express concern about the lack of such unifying Christmas traditions in modern America.
5. (   ) Penne Restad wrote a book "Christmas in America: A History."
6. (   ) Religion did not play a big role in how an American might celebrate the holiday.
7. (   ) By mid-century, Christian groups began to ignore their religious differences over the meaning of Christmas.
8. (   ) Christmas did not become an important time for families to celebrate at home.
9. (   ) As traditions increased in popularity, the modern trade and business linked to Christmas.
10. (   ) As Christmas became more popular, not states declared the day a state holiday.

Listening Comprehension Questions

次の英語を聴いて空欄を埋めてください．

http://learningenglish.voanews.com/audio/audio/345315.html

00:10-00:43

From VOA Learning English, welcome to The Making of a (   ), our (   ) program of American (   ) for people learning American English. I'm Steve Ember. Today Shirley Griffith and I (   ) a special program on (   ) (   ) in the United States during the (   ) (   ) of the (   ) (   ).

English Composition

次の日本文を英文に直してください．

1. 1819年，アメリカ人作家のワシントン・アービングは一冊の本を出版した．（publish を使って）

___

2. 多くの移民が彼らの母国からクリスマスの伝統を持ち込んだ．（bring を使って）

___

3. クリスマスは家庭で祝う家族にとって重要な時間となった．（become, celebrate を使って）

___

ひとくちコラム

　アメリカでは，イエス・キリストの生誕を祝う12月25日（Christmas Day）は国民の休日となっている．アメリカ国立議会図書館（Library of Congress）はホームページ上で"America's Story"として"Christmas Day"の項目を設けて説明している．キリスト教徒の多くの家庭ではクリスマスツリーを飾り，プレゼントを用意し，クリスマスを祝う．国民の休日のため，クリスマス商戦で賑わうショッピングモールは別として，交通機関は休日ダイヤとなり，クリスマスを祝うために学校や政府機関，企業は休日となる．日本では，クリスマスは休日とならない．アメリカの場合，少なくともキリスト教徒の間では休日のクリスマスを各家庭で厳かに祝うという雰囲気がある．

Unit 14　　　　　　　　　　　　　　　　　　　　Economy

Americans Celebrate Thanksgiving by Eating, Serving and ... Shopping?

http://learningenglish.voanews.com/a/2313139.html

出典：VOA, Public Domain
http://gdb.voanews.com/C1A4FD7B-F10F-421C-8E2A-6758C422F749_w640_r1_s.jpg

(00:49-05:14)

1　　The writer O. Henry called Thanksgiving the one day that is purely American. Thanksgiving is not a religious holiday. But it has spiritual meaning. Some Americans attend religious services on the day before Thanksgiving, or on Thanksgiving morning.

5　　Others travel great distances to be with their families. They have a large dinner, which is the main part of the celebration. For many Americans, Thanksgiving is the only time when all members of a family gather together. The holiday is a time of family reunion.

　　Thanksgiving is celebrated every year on the fourth Thursday of November.
10 The month of November is autumn in the United States. Autumn is the season when crops are gathered. When the first European settlers in America gathered their crops, they celebrated and gave thanks for the food. They thanked God for the success of the harvest. Many people continue to give thanks on the holiday, but it may not be for a good harvest.

15　　Sasha Bischoff is from Washington. This year, she says, she is thankful for her son Sebastian. "So Thanksgiving for me is about giving thanks, and really embracing loved ones and things. And this year, I am most thankful for my beloved son Sebastian, who just turned one."

Tradition says Pilgrim settlers from England celebrated the first Thanksgiving in 1621. There is evidence that settlers in other parts of America held earlier Thanksgiving celebrations. But the Pilgrims' Thanksgiving story is the most popular.

The Pilgrims were religious dissidents who fled oppression in England. They went first to the Netherlands. Then they left that country to establish a colony in North America. The Pilgrims landed in 1620 in what later became known as Plymouth, Massachusetts.

Their trip across the Atlantic Ocean was difficult. Their first months in America were difficult, too. About 100 Pilgrims landed just as autumn was turning to winter. During the cold months that followed, about half of them died.

When spring came, the Pilgrims began to plant crops. A Native American Indian named Squanto helped them. When summer ended, the Pilgrims had a good harvest of corn and barley. There was enough food to last through the winter.

The Pilgrims decided to hold a celebration to give thanks for their harvest. Writings from that time say Pilgrim leader William Bradford set a date late in the year. He invited members of a nearby Indian tribe to attend.

That Thanksgiving celebration lasted three days. There were many kinds of food. The meal included wild birds such as ducks, geese and turkeys. As the American colonies grew, many towns and settlements held Thanksgiving – or harvest – celebrations. Yet it was not until about 240 years later that a national day for Thanksgiving was declared.

読解のための語彙，文法および構文

p.71 ℓ.1 **O. Henry**: オー・ヘンリー（1862～1910年，アメリカの短編作家）
p.71 ℓ.1 **Thanksgiving**: 感謝祭，感謝祭の祝日
p.71 ℓ.1 **purely American**: 実にアメリカ的
p.71 ℓ.2 **religious holiday**: 宗教的な休日
p.71 ℓ.2 **spiritual meaning**: 霊的な意味
p.71 ℓ.3 **religious services**: 礼拝
p.71 ℓ.3 **on the day before Thanksgiving**: 感謝祭の前日
p.71 ℓ.5 **travel great distances**: 長距離を旅行する
p.71 ℓ.5 **large dinner**: 豪華な夕食

Unit 14　Americans Celebrate Thanksgiving by Eating, Serving and ... Shopping?　73

p.71 ℓ.6 p.72 ℓ.33	celebration:	お祝い，祝賀，祝典，称賛
p.71 ℓ.7	gather together:	集まる
p.71 ℓ.8	family reunion:	家族の新たな結びつき
p.71 ℓ.9	the fourth Thursday of November:	11月の第4木曜日
p.71 ℓ.10	autumn:	秋
p.71 ℓ.11	crops are gathered:	農作物が収穫される
p.71 ℓ.11	the first European settlers in America:	アメリカに最初に来たヨーロッパからの移住者
p.71 ℓ.12	celebrated and gave thanks for the food:	食物の収穫を祝い，感謝を捧げた
p.71 ℓ.12	thank God for　:	～について神に感謝する
p.71 ℓ.14	good harvest:	豊作
p.71 ℓ.15	Sasha Bischoff:	サーシャ・バイショフ
p.71 ℓ.16	Sebastian:	セバスチャン
p.72 ℓ.17	embracing loved ones and things:	愛している者や物を抱きしめる
p.72 ℓ.19	tradition says:	伝承によると
p.72 ℓ.19	Pilgrim:	ピルグリム．メイフラワー号でアメリカに向けて出帆し，1620年にニューイングランドにプリマスの植民地を設立したイギリスからの移住民．彼らは「ピルグリム・ファーザーズ」(巡礼父祖)と呼ばれ，ピューリタン(清教徒)であった．
p.72 ℓ.23	dissidents:	反対意見の人，反対者，反体制の人
p.72 ℓ.23	fled　:	～から逃げる，～を逃れる
p.72 ℓ.23	oppression:	圧迫，圧制
p.72 ℓ.24	Netherlands:	オランダ
p.72 ℓ.24	establish a colony:	植民地を作った
p.72 ℓ.25	North America:	北米
p.72 ℓ.25	land:	上陸する
p.72 ℓ.26	Plymouth, Massachusetts:	マサチューセッツのプリマス
p.72 ℓ.27	trip across the Atlantic Ocean:	大西洋横断の旅
p.72 ℓ.28-29	turning to winter:	冬に移る
p.72 ℓ.29	cold months:	寒い数か月
p.72 ℓ.29	half of them died:	半数が亡くなった
p.72 ℓ.30	plant crops:	農作物を植える
p.72 ℓ.30-31	Native American Indian:	先住のアメリカンインディアン
p.72 ℓ.31	Squanto:	スカント
p.72 ℓ.32	corn:	トウモロコシ
p.72 ℓ.32	barley:	オオムギ

p.72 ℓ.34 William Bradford: ウィリアム・ブラッドフォード

p.72 ℓ.35 tribe: 部族，一族

p.72 ℓ.36 last: 続く

p.72 ℓ.37 meal: 食事

p.72 ℓ.37 wild bird: 野鳥

p.72 ℓ.37 duck: アヒル

p.72 ℓ.37 goose: ガチョウ

p.72 ℓ.37 turkey: シチメンチョウ

p.72 ℓ.38 settlements: 入植地

p.72 ℓ.39 national day: 国家的記念日

p.72 ℓ.40 declare: 宣言する

Reading Comprehension Questions

次の各文が，本文の内容に合っていればTを，合っていない場合はFを，括弧内に記入してください．

1. (　) The writer O. Henry called Christmas the one day that is purely American.
2. (　) Others travel great distances to be with their families on Thanksgiving.
3. (　) Thanksgiving is celebrated every year on the third Thursday of November.
4. (　) This year, Ms. Sasha Bischoff is most thankful for her beloved son.
5. (　) Tradition says Pilgrim settlers from England celebrated the first Thanksgiving in 1600.
6. (　) The Pilgrims were religious dissidents who fled oppression in England.
7. (　) Their Pilgrims' trip across the Atlantic Ocean was easy.
8. (　) When spring came, the Pilgrims began to plant crops.
9. (　) The Pilgrims decided to hold a celebration to give thanks for their harvest.
10. (　) The meal did not include wild birds such as ducks, geese and turkeys.

Unit 14 Americans Celebrate Thanksgiving by Eating, Serving and ... Shopping? 75

Listening Comprehension Questions

次の英語を聴いて空欄を埋めてください．

http://learningenglish.voanews.com/audio/audio/348402.html

00:06-00:47

Welcome to This Is America from VOA Learning English. I'm Steve Ember. And I'm Kelly Jean Kelly. (　　　) the smell of sliced apples and spices like cinnamon and ginger all (　　　) (　　　) and (　　　). Then let everything (　　　) (　　　) and add a little sugar on top. For many Americans, that smell — the smell of apple pie — is a favorite part of (　　　) Day. Today we (　　　) on the history of the holiday and how Americans (　　　) (　　　) this year.

English Composition

次の日本文を英文に直してください．

1. 作家のオー・ヘンリーは感謝祭の祝日を実にアメリカ的な一日と呼んだ．（call を使って）

　_____

2. 感謝祭は毎年 11 月の第 4 木曜日に祝われる．（be celebrated を使って）

　_____

3. 春が来ると，ピルグリムたちは農作物を植え始めた．（plant を使って）

　_____

ひとくちコラム

　アメリカでは 11 月の第 4 木曜日が感謝祭であり，国民の休日となる．感謝祭は課題文で説明された歴史を持つ．シカゴ大学図書館では，感謝祭に関する七面鳥についてのリサーチガイドを公開している．取り上げられているトピックは，アメリカ史における七面鳥，七面鳥料理，七面鳥の経済など動画資料も含めた構成になっている．現在アメリカでは感謝祭の翌日は休日ではないが「ブラック・フライデー」と呼ばれ，大バーゲンが行われる．クリスマス商戦が開始される日で，アメリカで最も多くの人々が買い物をする日と言われている．

Unit 15

Ethnic

New Study: Foreign Students Make U.S. Better, Faster

http://learningenglish.voanews.com/a/2310080.html

出典：VOA, Public Domain
http://gdb.voanews.com/C69AD11A-C382-4231-B5C6-42C6263EF5EB_w640_r1_s_cx0_cy6_cw0.jpg

(00:21-03:55)

1   Many of them celebrate a young woman's quinceañera—that is, her 15th birthday. But first, we talk about foreign students in the United States. A new report says the government should make it easier for foreigners working toward high-level degrees to stay in the country. Mario Ritter has this report from VOA's
5 Joe DeCapua.

   The United States educates many foreign students, especially in areas like science and engineering. But what do international students add to the country after they finish their study programs?

   Three economists decided to investigate. The head of the team was Keith
10 Maskus, a professor at the University of Colorado in Boulder. He says after the terrorist attacks of September 11, 2001, the U.S. made it much harder for students from some parts of the world to enter graduate programs.

   At the time, many American officials and educators warned that limiting foreign students would harm scientific development and innovation. "And I
15 thought, well, that's very interesting, but do we really know if that's true?"

   Professor Maskus worked on the study with Ahmed Mushfiq Mobarak of

Yale and Eric Stuen of the University of Idaho. The three men gathered data—a lot of data. They studied over 75,000 Ph.D students in the top U.S. science and engineering universities from the late 1970s to the late 1990s.

20　　They found that diversity improved productivity and efficiency. In other words, a mix of American and foreign students made schools and workplaces better and faster.

"It seems to have something to do with the fact that networks and laboratory sciences [are] really a function of how the graduate students and the post-
25 doctoral students and everyone else can specialize in some element of science-and also the fact that their undergraduate training and possibly some graduate training in whatever it is-mathematics or bench science or laboratory science-gives them different approaches to thinking about problems.

"And when these people can get together and bounce ideas off each other the
30 sort of outcome of that is more dynamic intellectual process. And you get more ideas with having some diversity like that."

Professor Maskus says his group's findings suggest that the U.S. should change its policies toward foreign students. Right now, students have to demonstrate that they or their family has enough money to pay for their education, even if schools
35 offer aid.

He also says the government should make it easier for foreign students to get green cards so they can live permanently in the United States. He notes that countries like Canada and Australia let international students with Ph.Ds in science, technology or engineering become permanent residents. But the
40 United States requires students who want to remain in the country to find a local employer who will give them a temporary visa.

読解のための語彙，文法および構文

- *p.76 ℓ.1*　a young woman's quinceañera:（スペイン語で）15歳になった少女の誕生日
- *p.76 ℓ.2*　foreign students: 外国人留学生
- *p.76 ℓ.3* / *p.77 ℓ.36*　make it easier: 簡素化する，簡単にする
- *p.76 ℓ.3-4*　working toward high-level degrees: 高い学位を取得するために取り組む
- *p.76 ℓ.4*　Mario Ritter: マリオ・リッター
- *p.76 ℓ.5*　Joe DeCapua: ジョー・デカプア
- *p.76 ℓ.6*　educate: 教育する
- *p.76 ℓ.7*　science and engineering: 科学技術

p.76 ℓ.7	international students:	外国人留学生
p.76 ℓ.8	finish their study programs:	教育課程を修了する
p.76 ℓ.9	economists:	経済学者
p.76 ℓ.9	investigate:	調査する
p.76 ℓ.9-10	Keith Maskus:	キース・マスカス
p.76 ℓ.10	University of Colorado:	コロラド大学
p.76 ℓ.10	Boulder:	ボールダー
p.76 ℓ.11	terrorist attacks:	テロ攻撃
p.76 ℓ.11	September 11, 2001:	アメリカで起きた同時多発テロ事件は，アメリカ合衆国で発生した，航空機を使った4つのテロ事件の総称である．この大規模なテロ事件が起きた日時が2001年9月11日だった．
p.76 ℓ.12	enter graduate programs:	博士課程に入学する
p.76 ℓ.13	at the time:	当時
p.76 ℓ.13	many American officials:	多くのアメリカ官庁職員
p.76 ℓ.13	educators:	教育者
p.76 ℓ.13	warn:	警告する
p.76 ℓ.14	harm scientific development and innovation:	科学の発達や革新が損なわれる
p.76 ℓ.16	Ahmed Mushfiq Mobarak:	アームド・マスフィク・ムバラク
p.77 ℓ.17	Yale:	イェール大学
p.77 ℓ.17	Eric Stuen:	エリック・スタン
p.77 ℓ.17	University of Idaho:	アイダホ大学
p.77 ℓ.18	Ph.D students:	博士課程の大学院生
p.77 ℓ.19	late 1970s:	1970年代後半
p.77 ℓ.20	diversity:	多様性
p.77 ℓ.20	productivity:	生産性
p.77 ℓ.20	efficiency:	効率性
p.77 ℓ.20-21	in other words:	言い換えると，
p.77 ℓ.21	workplaces:	職場
p.77 ℓ.23	networks:	ネットワーク
p.77 ℓ.23-24	laboratory sciences:	実験室の科学
p.77 ℓ.24	graduate students:	大学院生
p.77 ℓ.24-25	post-doctoral students:	博士号を有する学生
p.77 ℓ.25	specialize in:	専攻する
p.77 ℓ.26	undergraduate training:	学部の勉学
p.77 ℓ.26	graduate training:	大学院での研究

p.77 ℓ.27	mathematics:	数学
p.77 ℓ.27	bench science:	実験の科学
p.77 ℓ.28	approaches:	アプローチ
p.77 ℓ.29	bounce ideas off each other:	互いにアイデアを引き出す
p.77 ℓ.30	outcome of ：	～の結果
p.77 ℓ.30	dynamic intellectual process:	ダイナミックな思考過程
p.77 ℓ.32	suggest:	示唆する
p.77 ℓ.33	policies toward foreign students:	外国人留学生に対する政策
p.77 ℓ.33	demonstrate:	示す
p.77 ℓ.34	pay for:	支払う
p.77 ℓ.37	get green cards:	グリーンカード（永住者カード）を取得する
p.77 ℓ.37	live permanently in the United States:	アメリカに永住する
p.77 ℓ.39	permanent resident:	永住者
p.77 ℓ.40	remain in the country:	国に残る
p.77 ℓ.40-41	local employer:	地元の雇用者
p.77 ℓ.41	temporary visa:	短期ビザ

Reading Comprehension Questions

次の各文が，本文の内容に合っていればTを，合っていない場合はFを，括弧内に記入してください．

1. (　) A new report says the government should make it easier for foreigners working toward high-level degrees to stay in the country.
2. (　) The United States doesn't educate many foreign students, especially in areas like science and engineering.
3. (　) Two economists decided to investigate.
4. (　) Many American officials and educators did not warn that limiting foreign students would harm scientific development and innovation.
5. (　) Professor Maskus worked on the study with Ahmed Mushfiq Mobarak and Eric Stuen.
6. (　) They found that diversity improved productivity and efficiency.
7. (　) Professor Maskus says his group's findings suggest that the U.S. should not change its policies.
8. (　) Right now, students have to demonstrate that they or their family has enough money to pay for their education.

9. (　　) Professor Maskus says the government should make it easier for foreign students to get green cards.

10. (　　) Canada and Australia do not let international students with Ph.Ds in science, technology or engineering become permanent residents

Listening Comprehension Questions

次の英語を聴いて空欄を埋めてください．

http://learningenglish.voanews.com/audio/audio/345326.html

00:03-00:20

Welcome back to As It Is. Today we will (　　) (　　　　) (　　　) people who (　　　) (　　) the United States from other countries. Some are immigrants who (　　　　) their traditions with them. On our show, we (　　　　) (　　) families from (　　　) (　　　　　) nations.

English Composition

次の日本文を英文に直してください．

1. 私たちはアメリカに滞在している外国人留学生について話をします．（talk about を使って）

2. 彼らは多様性が生産性と効率性を改善することに気づいた．（find を使って）

3. アメリカは外国人留学生に対する政策を変更するべきである．（change を使って）

ひとくちコラム

　アメリカ国際教育協会（IIE）によると，2011～2012年における中国からの留学生はおよそ19万4,000人で，留学生総数に占める割合は25.4％となっている．次はインドからの留学生およそ10万人で，留学生総数に占める割合は13.1％である．日本からはおよそ2万人でアメリカの留学生総数における割合は2.6％に過ぎない．現在の留学生の現状を見ると，今後アメリカの大学を卒業し，学位を授与され，活躍が最も期待される留学生は中国，インドなど東アジア圏からの留学生である．アメリカは留学生が学位取得後の就職などの整備を今後も行う予定である．これまでの日米関係を鑑み，今後の良好な日米関係のためにも日本人留学生の活躍を期待したい．

訳例と解答

Unit 1. ダイエットは大きなビジネスになる
【訳例】

またあの時期が来る．温暖な気候が北半球に戻ってきた．夏になると人々は水着姿になり，近くのプールや海辺で泳ぎたくなる．だが，まずは冬期間に増えた体重を減らすのが厄介なのだ．

私たちの多くは冬期間の運動不足のために体重が増える．海水浴をする前に余分な体重を落とそうと極端なことをする者もいる．ダイエット産業では体重を減らすアイデアが尽きることは絶対にない．

睡眠が体重を減らすという就寝ダイエットを考えてみよう．このダイエット方法は，睡眠中は物を食べられないという理論から成っている．そしてサナダムシダイエットがある．サナダムシが寄生していると，人間の腹部にたまっている食べ物をサナダムシが摂取してダイエットに役立つという．しかし，このダイエット法では最初に寄生虫を飲み込まなければならない．これはダイエットよりも深刻な問題である．

奇妙で目新しいダイエット，ダイエット療法，エクササイズ方法が毎日のように市場に出回る．それらは体重を減少させ，水着姿が美しく映える肉体を手に入れることを約束する．ダイエット産業は毎年何十億ドルもの収益があり，成長している．あるリサーチ会社の調査によると，ダイエット業界は，2015年までに世界で6,700億ドル規模になると見られている．

マーケット・アンド・マーケットによると，ダイエット産業は3大分野で構成されているという．それは，減量サービス，フィジカル・フィットネスと美容整形，最後が飲食物である．ダイエットのアイデア供給は尽きることがないように見える．カロリーを抑え，好きなだけ食べられる低炭水化物食や低脂肪食がある．何千種類もの痩せ薬やダイエット方法がある．

どこから始めるとよいのか．何が最適な方法なのか．専門家によると，万人にとって最良の方法は1つではないという．多くの専門家が一致している見解は，体重を減らすには摂取カロリー以上のカロリーを消費または燃焼させる必要があるということだ．体が必要としている以上のカロリーを摂取すると，脂肪として余分なエネルギーが蓄えられる．

カロリーは食物のエネルギーの尺度である．1ポンドの脂肪は453グラムの脂肪または3,500カロリーに相当する．1週間でその脂肪を減らすためには少なくともそれと同じだけのカロリーを燃焼させるか，食べ物を減らさなければならない．最良の方法は双方のアイデアを組み合わせることである．カロリーの少ない物を摂取し，運動を増やし，さらにカロリーを燃焼させればよいのである．

アメリカ国立衛生研究所は，医学的管理が無くても，女性は一日におよそ1,200カロリーに摂取を制限することを提案している．また男性はおよそ1,500カロリーに摂取を制限するべきであるという．今後もカロリー要件を満たす最良の方法について議論は続くだろう．

【Reading Comprehension Questions 解答】
1. T 2. F 3. T 4. F 5. T 6. T 7. F 8. T 9. F 10. T

【Listening Comprehension Questions 解答】
(This) is Science in the (News) in VOA Special English. I'm Shirley Griffith. And I'm Bob Doughty. (Today) we will talk about diet and weight loss. (Exercise) is important if you want to get in good shape. But (experts) say exercise alone is not enough if your goal is to lose (weight).

【English Composition 解答】
1. Warm weather has returned to Earth's northern hemisphere.
2. Many of us gain weight because of inactivity during the winter.
3. The weight loss industry takes in billions of dollars each year.

Unit 2. サイレントキラー：一酸化炭素中毒
【訳例】
　今月初め，中国人男性2人がネパールのホテルの一室で死亡しているのが発見された．検視した医師がフランス通信社（AFP）に伝えた．検視官によると，ガスストーブの不具合による一酸化炭素中毒死だった．地元の警察署はホテルの部屋の汚れた空気の流れも一酸化炭素中毒死の一因であると述べている．
　12月には，警察官がコロラド州コマースシティに住むアメリカ人コミュニティーの一家庭から呼び出された．警察官らは，男性がひとり死亡し，他の7人が一酸化炭素中毒症状で苦しんでいるのを発見した．その7人は治療のため病院に運ばれた．
　以上が今月世界で報告された一酸化炭素中毒の事例2件である．アメリカの疾病対策予防センター（CDC）によると，一酸化炭素中毒で毎年何百人もの人々が死亡し，何千人もの人々が体調不良を起こしている．
　CDCは，一酸化炭素中毒は屋外の新鮮な空気の中でも起きると指摘している．CDCによると，一酸化炭素は発電機やハウスボートのエンジンなどと関係がある．
　消費者製品安全委員会は何千もの製品による不慮の死や怪我のリスクからアメリカ国民を守る責任がある．委員会は死亡記録を調査し，管理下の製品による一酸化炭素中毒関連の死亡者数を概算した．
　死亡者数を検索できる最近の年度は2009年で，この年には146人が死亡した．死亡者の53パーセントは発電機のようなエンジン駆動の装置による死亡だった．暖房装置による死亡は27パーセントだった．その他は木炭使用のグリルや給湯器，ランタンが原因の死亡だった．
　一酸化炭素中毒はアメリカで問題になっているだけではない．世界中で多くの人々や動物が一酸化炭素中毒で死亡し，体調不良になっている．一酸化炭素は人々が最初に，食べ物を調理する

ためや暖をとるために燃料を燃やし始めてから問題になっている．寒い気象となる世界のあらゆる場所で起きる問題なのである．一酸化炭素が，空中を漂っていることに人々が気づかないため，サイレントキラーと呼ばれている．一酸化炭素は無色である．無味である．そして無臭である．一酸化炭素が原因で燃焼する光景が目に映るわけではない．一酸化炭素は人々が咳き込む原因にもならない．しかし命に関わるのだ．一酸化炭素は素早く血中に入り込み，酸素を取り込む能力を奪ってしまう．

　一酸化炭素は，血液が身体組織に酸素を運ぶ能力を低下させる．血中に溶け込んで能力低下を引き起こす．一酸化炭素が血中に溶け込むと，血液は酸素を必要とする身体の組織にもはや酸素を送れなくなってしまうのである．

【Reading Comprehension Questions 解答】
1．F　2．T　3．T　4．F　5．F　6．T　7．T　8．F　9．T　10．F

【Listening Comprehension Questions 解答】
I'm Bob Doughty. And I'm June Simms.（Winter）（has）（brought）cold weather to many parts of Earth's northern（hemisphere）. With the cold（comes）a danger as old as our knowledge of fire -- death or injury by（carbon）（monoxide）（poisoning）. Today, we（tell）（about）this ancient and continuing danger.

【English Composition 解答】
1. Two Chinese men were found dead in their hotel room in Nepal earlier this month.
2. The seven were taken to a hospital for treatment.
3. Carbon monoxide decreases the ability of the blood to carry oxygen to body tissues.

Unit 3. 科学技術の発明が命を救う
【訳例】
　ほとんどの車にはシートベルトが装置の一部として装着されている．シートベルトは事故が起きると，運転手と乗員を守る．安全専門家は，拘束具であるシートベルトはアメリカ内だけでも何千人もの命を救ってきたと見ている．世界規模ではシートベルトで救われた人々は百万人にもおよぶ．

　最初のシートベルトは1800年代にイギリスのジョージ・ケイリーが製作したと言われている．彼は多くの物を発明したが，特に初期の「空飛ぶ機械」を発明したことで知られている．

　アメリカでは，1849年に自動車のシートベルトが発明されている．アメリカ政府はニューヨーク市に住むエドワード・J・クレイグホーンに特許を与え，他の人々が彼の発明を複製できないようにした．クレイグホーンはその装置を安全ベルトと名付けた．その安全ベルトは固定装置に

人を固定するためにフックと他の付属品でできた装置だった．

　他の発明者は別のシートベルトを製作した．しかし，世間で広く使われている現在のシートベルトが開発されるまで 100 年超かかった．現在使われているシートベルトはスウェーデンの技術者ニルス・ブリン氏が製作した．膝から肩まで 3 点を支えるシートベルトは，50 年前にヨーロッパで初めて乗用車に装着された．

　ブリン氏は 1920 年にスウェーデンで生まれた．大学を卒業後，彼はスウェーデンの航空機業界で航空機の座席を設計した．その座席はパイロットが事故の際に脱出するために製造された．ブリン氏の航空機座席の取り組みで高速で衝突する時に何が起きるのかが判明した．1958 年ブリン氏はその知識をスウェーデンの車両製造会社であるボルボ社に提供した．彼はボルボ社で最初の安全担当技師主任となった．

　当時，最も安全な車のシートベルトは腹部で交差していた．ベルトのバックルが定位置に体を固定した．しかし，ひどい衝突事故の場合は，バックルの位置がしばしば重症を負う原因ともなった．

　ブリン氏は，身体の上部，下部の双方を安全に装置に固定する必要があると理解した．彼の発明は布製のストラップが胸部に掛かり，他のストラップが臀部に掛かるシートベルトだった．そのデザインは臀部の近くでストラップがつながっていた．

　ボルボ社は車に固定する現在のシートベルトを最初に採用した車両会社である．ニルス・ブリン氏のデザインの使用を他の車両メーカーにも提供している．

　スウェーデンの技術者であるブリン氏は自らが発明したシートベルトで名声を得た．彼は 1995 年にスウェーデン王立科学アカデミーから金メダルを授与された．2002 年スウェーデンでその生涯を閉じた．

　ケブラーは多くの人々を重傷や死から救うもう 1 つの発明である．ケブラーは繊維素材で，弾丸をはねつける性質を持っている．衣類に装着されたこの素材は，世界中で警官や兵士らを守っている．

　繊維は銃撃から身体を保護するバリアになる．弾丸はケブラーに当たると形が崩れる．ケブラーに当たった弾丸はキノコ状になり，身体の中に入らなくなる．警察や公安担当職員にとっての脅威のほとんどは拳銃によるものである．彼らは上半身を保護するために防弾チョッキを身につける．兵士らは重火器攻撃に備え，さらに広範囲にケブラーで保護された衣類を身につける．

【Reading Comprehension Questions 解答】
1. T　2. F　3. F　4. T　5. T　6. F　7. T　8. F　9. F　10. T

【Listening Comprehension Questions 解答】
This is (Science) in the News, in VOA Special English. I'm June Simms. Today Shirley Griffith and Bob Doughty (tell) (about) two (recent) (inventions) that (have) (helped) to (save) (lives). We will also tell about the people who (developed) them.

【English Composition 解答】
1. Seat belts protect drivers and passengers in case of accident.
2. Claghorn called the device a Safety-Belt.
3. At the time, most safety belts in cars crossed the body over the abdomen.

Unit 4. 南北戦争：だれが記念樹を植えるべきか
【訳例】

　南北戦争はアメリカ史上，最も悲惨な戦争である．1861年から1865年まで少なくとも62万人の兵士がその戦争で死亡した．南北戦争は，主に奴隷制の問題をめぐり南部諸州が北部とのつながりを断ったことから始まった．南部の州は独立を宣言し，南部同盟として知られている南部連合国を作った．150年後の現在，戦死者を祀るために生きた記念樹を植えることになった．ジム・テダーがそのプロジェクトについて詳細を説明する．

　非営利団体であるジャーニー・スルー・ハロード・グランドは奮闘している．南北戦争で戦死した各兵士のために植樹を行い，現在生えている木も記念樹とする計画を立てている．記念樹は4州およそ300キロに渡る道路に植樹する予定である．植樹は南北戦争が勃発したペンシルバニア州のゲティスバーグから始まる．そして，第3代米国大統領トマス・ジェファーソンの故郷であるバージニア州のシャーロットビルで終了する．

　ベス・エリクソンはジャーニー・スルー・ハロード・グランドとこの事業に取り組んでいる．「人々はこれらの木を見るたびに，影響を受けるでしょう」．最初の植樹が11月，広大で歴史のあるバージニア州のオートランズと呼ばれる農場で行われた．歴史トラストは元プランテーションを所有している．

　アンドレア・マクジムシーはオートランズの専務理事である．彼女は，この元プランテーションは植樹を始めるのには良い場所だと言っている．「オートランズにはかなり古い南北戦争の頃からの木があります．多くの木々は植樹プロジェクトの一部として実際に使用される予定です」．彼女は，オートランズは南北戦争跡地の一部だと付け加えた．「オートランズには，南北戦争が始まる直前の1860年に128名の奴隷がいました．この土地に住んでいた家族の2人の息子は南軍に従軍しました」．

　リチャード・ウィリアムは現在オートランズに住む家族の一員である．彼の家族は家に隣接した土地を所有している．植樹プロジェクトにも参加している．「民間の地主としてわれわれは，このプロジェクトが大成功し，他の民間地主の参加を促すことができるよう希望しています」．

　植樹プロジェクトに対する民間の寄付は6,500万ドルが期待されている．寄付金額は植樹1本につき100ドルである．植樹は特にスマートフォンユーザーにとっては興味深いものとなるだろう．特別マークを付けると，ユーザーは木と南北戦争で戦った個々の兵士の物語を結びつけることができる．

　ベス・エリクソンは説明する．「これらの木に個人とつながる番号を付けることができます．

GPS機能を使ってだれの木かを知ることができるのです」．

　エレノア・アダムズ氏は彼女の祖先であるジョセフ・マクゴワン氏に敬意を表して木を1本寄付した．ジョセフ・マクゴワン氏はアラバマ出身で南部のために戦った．彼は23歳で銃弾に倒れ亡くなった．アダムズ氏は，この若き兵士が家族宛の手紙で戦場の日々について書いている．「彼は病気，夏の暑さ，食糧事情の悪さについて綴っています．当時兵士でいることは本当に大変だったのです．」彼女は自分の家族が南北戦争で亡くなったマクゴワン家の人々のために植樹してほしいと考えている．

【Reading Comprehension Questions 解答】
1．T　2．T　3．F　4．F　5．T　6．F　7．T　8．F　9．T　10．F

【Listening Comprehension Questions 解答】
（Welcome）to AMERICAN MOSAIC, in VOA Special English.
I'm June Simms. On the show today, we（hear）music from some of the performers at the South by Southwest music festival in Austin, Texas. We（talk）（about）efforts to（remember）the many Americans（killed）in the nation's Civil War in the 1860s. And we（tell）（about）efforts against some of the Civil War memorials that already（exist）.

【English Composition 解答】
1. At least 620,000 soldiers died in the fighting.
2. The southern states declared independence.
3. Private donations are expected to pay for the 65 million dollar tree planting project.

Unit 5. 農家は新たな農作物生産方法を発明
【訳例】
　ブレイク・ウィズナント氏と家族は農家を経営してきた．彼の家族はアメリカのフロリダ州に住んでいる．100年近く，ウィズナント家は果物と野菜を栽培し，世界中の企業に販売してきた．中央フロリダの温暖な気候は農作物，特にトマトを栽培するのに適している．同氏が800ヘクタールの土地で栽培してきたのはトマトである．

　1992年ウィズナント氏は不運に見舞われた．雨が降り始めた．そして降り続いた．さらに降った．50センチに達しようとする雨水がその年のトマトを台無しにした．ウィズナント氏は苦境に陥った．

　「私は，考えました．もっと良い方法を考案しなければならないとね」．

　彼はこの惨事が決して起こらぬような方策を立て始めた．同氏は下から農作物に水を供給する方法を開発したかった．彼はカバーのようなものが雨を防ぎ，土を暖めると考えた．ほとんどス

ペースを使わない箱の中で農作物を育てたかった．同氏はその考えにとりつかれ，四六時中それを考えていた．

「私は妻に言いました．死ぬまでに地面の上に箱を組み立て，その中でトマトが育つのを見たいと．」何年もその作業に取り組んだ後，彼はどうすべきかが分かった．

彼はペンシルバニア州で箱を作ることに賛同してくれる会社を見つけた．厚いプラスチックでできたものだった．長さがおよそ1メートル，奥行きが50センチだった．箱の中には給水用のプラスチック管と多くの穴が開けられたプラスチックの仕切りがついていた．

土ではなく箱の底部にある水を上方にためるピートモスのような物質が，箱内の仕切りの上に設置された．雨水と害虫を防ぐために薄いプラスチックカバーが箱の上部に取り付けられた．ブレイクはこの箱をアースボックスと呼んだ．

フランク・ディパオロ氏は，ペンシルバニア州スクラントンにあるアースボックス・カンパニーの部長である．彼はコンテナー・ガーデニングと呼ばれている方法で野菜を育てることで，ブレイク・ウィズナントや他の農業従事者が農作物を育てる時の共通問題を即座に解決することができると言っている．

「彼は農場の中で農作物に病気や問題の類が起きると一人の人間が基本的にそこへ行き，他の農作物に害が広がらないよう，ボックスを担当し，農場の問題を取り除くだけで良いのです」．

ディパオロ氏は，通常の泥や土はこのコンテナー・ガーデニングには適さないと述べている．代わりに苗床用にミックスした土が使われる．これはほとんどがピートモスで，作物の根に空気を取り込みやすくするために添加物を施している．

「コンテナー・ガーデニングの責任の1つは農作物に水をやることなのです．ちょっとした小さな苗木を植えると，根は水の容器に届くほど長く根を張っていません．ですからその苗に水が届くようにする必要があるのです」．

【Reading Comprehension Questions 解答】

1. F　2. T　3. T　4. F　5. T　6. F　7. T　8. F　9. F　10. T

【Listening Comprehension Questions 解答】

From VOA Learning English, this is（Science）in the News.（Today），we（tell）（about）an American farmer and an unusual device he（developed）. For（20）years, people around the world（have）（been）（buying）his（invention）.

【English Composition 解答】

1. In 1992, Mr. Whisenant had some bad luck.

2. He found a company in Pennsylvania that agreed to make the box.

3. Blake called it, the EarthBox.

Unit 6. ハミルトン，新たな国家のために中央銀行制度を模索
【訳例】

　アレクサンダー・ハミルトンは，どんな国家も工業化なくては近代国家を作ることはできないと固く信じていた．だから，彼はアメリカを工業国にする計画を慎重に発展させていった．

　彼の計画の一部はアメリカの製造業者を外国の強豪相手から保護するものだった．ハミルトンはアメリカの港に運び込まれた数種の外国製品には輸入税をかけるシステムを確立することで国内の製造業者を保護した．この関税によって外国製品の価格は高くなった．結果として，アメリカの製造業者が製品を販売する際に競合相手が少なくなった．

　ハミルトンはまた，国家の財政を体系づけた．彼が行った最初の方策は，独立戦争時からの国家の負債を返済することだった．しかし彼はさらに進めたかった．国立銀行を創設する希望をいだいていたのである．

　ハミルトンは多くのヨーロッパ諸国が国立銀行を設立していると論じた．バージニア大学歴史学のアンドリュー・オショネシー教授によると，ハミルトンはイギリスの財政システムが優れていると考えていた．イギリスの財政システムは，小国も戦時には借款を行うことができるというシステムだった．

　「イギリスは，非常に効率的な金融システムと借入システムのおかげで，本質的に自国の規模よりもはるかに大きい権力のイメージを醸し出すことができる」．ハミルトンは，アメリカが国立銀行を創設すれば国内資金の流れが高まると述べた．それが政府の借款交渉や，税金の取り立てに役立つ可能性があった．経営史家であるジョン・スティール・ゴードンによると，ハミルトンは中央銀行の創設により州同士が競争するのを避けることができると信じていた．

　「銀行はマネービジネスの真っ只中に位置し，貸し過ぎや投機しすぎる問題を常に抱えている．だから彼は中央銀行のメカニズムで州の銀行を規制したかったのだ」．

　しかし，ハミルトンの計画は過去の脅威を呼び起こした．それは特に南部の農家間で強かった．批評家らは，国立銀行が北部の少数の富豪に特権を与えるのではないかと論じた．国立銀行が，南部農家や中小企業経営者らが頼っている州立銀行を規制する可能性もあった．金や銀を使う代わりに紙幣が増えると考えられた．

　ジェームズ・マディソンは議会でハミルトンの計画に対して率先して反対意見を述べた．マディソンは，合衆国は一箇所に富を集中させるべきではないと述べた．だから彼は多くの小規模銀行を国内のいたるところに設置するシステムを提案した．彼は，中央銀行構想は違憲であると論じた．

　アメリカの憲法についてジェームズ・マディソンよりも知る者はいなかった．彼は憲法の理念を知るものとして信頼されていた．だれもが彼の憲法講釈を尊敬していた．

　マディソンは，憲法は議会に多くの権力を与えていることを明記していると注釈した．たとえば，憲法は議会に資金を借り入れる権限を与えているのである．しかし議会は，債務の返済，国を守る，国民の一般財を提供するという時のみしか資金を借り入れることができなかった．マディソンは，憲法に記載されているよりも多くのことが行えるよう議会に許可を与えるのは危険

であると述べた.

【Reading Comprehension Questions 解答】
1. F 2. T 3. T 4. F 5. T 6. F 7. T 8. F 9. F 10. T

【Listening Comprehension Questions 解答】
From VOA Learning English, welcome to The (Making) of a (Nation) – (American) (history) in VOA Special English. I'm Steve Ember. (This) (week) in our series we (continue) the story of Alexander Hamilton. He was the nation's (first) (secretary) of the (treasury).

【English Composition 解答】
1. Hamilton carefully developed a program that would make the United States an industrial nation.
2. Hamilton also organized the nation's finances.
3. Madison said the United States should not put all its wealth in one place.

Unit 7. アダムズ大統領は米仏戦争を回避
【訳例】

　アダムズは聡明な人間だった．彼は愛国者であり有能な外交官だった．しかし政党政治が好きではなかった．彼の政党政治嫌いは大統領就任時期に問題となった．二大政党が彼の大統領就任期間に権力争いをしたからである．アダムズは争いの矢面に立たされた．

　ジョン・アダムズは連邦党の党員だった．彼は大統領であり，連邦党の党首だった．しかし，党首の地位は政治権力をどう得て何に使うかに長けたアレクサンダー・ハミルトンのような人物に当てはまるものだった．

　ハミルトンはワシントン大統領の下で財務長官として勤務した．その後ハミルトンは民間人となり，ニューヨーク市の弁護士として働いていた．しかし，彼は国政に大きな影響力を持ち続けた．連邦党員のハミルトンに対する忠誠心は議会も支配していた．

　アダムズ大統領の閣僚トップでさえもハミルトンに忠実だった．実際，彼らは新大統領であるアダムズに対し，そろって反目していたのである．この政治状況はアダムズの大統領職遂行を難しいものにしていた．これは連邦党の統治の終わりも意味していた．

　ジョン・ファーリング教授は，ウェスト・ジョージア大学歴史学の名誉教授である．アメリカ建国期に関する書籍を多く出版している．ファーリング教授によると，アメリカはおよそ半世紀ごとに一党独裁の極端な時期を経験してきた．1700年代後半は，特にそういう時代であった．党派心は連邦党の分裂の一因となった．

　「ハミルトンの派閥はウルトラ・フェデラリストまたはハイ・フェデラリストと呼ばれ，当時は中道主義の党員と争っていました．実際それが原因で連邦党は崩壊しました．連邦党は，1800

年の選挙に大敗後，存続できなかったのです」．

　アダムズの大統領就任時期には2つの大きな問題があった．第一に外交政策であり，第二に市民権の問題だった．まずはアメリカとフランスの関係だった．アメリカ人はフランスで起きた革命を支持するか否かで分裂した．最初は，多くがイギリスと対立したアメリカ独立戦争に似ていると見ていた．副大統領のトマス・ジェファーソンは特にフランスを支持した．

　フランスはアメリカがイギリスからの独立戦争に勝利するよう支援した．両国の友好関係はトマス・ジェファーソンが駐フランス公使の時も続いた．

　しかし，多くの連邦党員がフランス革命に強く反対するようになった．彼らはフランス王と女王の処刑に愕然としたのである．一般大衆が権力を掌握することを好まなかった．連邦党員らはイギリスとの同盟を望んだ．やがて彼らはフランスとの戦争を要求した．彼らはアメリカ政府がフランス支持の代表を送ることを阻止するために権力を駆使した．連邦党員は開戦の理由となる侮辱の兆候を探していた．

　ジョン・ファーリング教授によると，アダムズ大統領は大半の連邦党員に同意しなかった．「アダムズは最初から，いわゆる名誉ある講和を望んでいたのです．彼はいわゆる中間の位置，つまり右派の急進的な保守主義と左派の急進的な自由主義の間にいる中道主義の立場を模索していたのです」．

【Reading Comprehension Questions 解答】
1. F　2. T　3. F　4. T　5. T　6. F　7. T　8. F　9. F　10. T

【Listening Comprehension Questions 解答】
From VOA Learning English, welcome to The Making of a Nation. American history in Special English. I'm Steve Ember. This week in our series, we (continue) the (story) of America's second president, John Adams. He (took) (office) in (1797). He (had) (served) eight years as vice president under President (George) (Washington). Now, state electors had chosen him to (govern) the new nation.

【English Composition 解答】
1. Adams did not like party politics.
2. Hamilton had served as treasury secretary under President Washington.
3. Americans were divided on whether to support the revolution in France.

Unit 8. アメリカの貧困水準 1993年以来最悪
【訳例】
　アメリカの景気後退は2007年12月から2009年6月まで続いた．2007年には貧困率は2.5%超も上がった．新しい知見はワシントンDCのホームレス連合のマイケル・フェレル氏にとって

は驚きだった．

ファレル氏「近い将来，経済の方向転換がなければ，状況はさらに悪くなる可能性があります」．

国勢調査局によると，中位の家計収入は 2009 年から 2010 年までに 2% 超下落している．中位という意味は損得どちらも半ばで収入を得ているという意味である．前年度は，中位家計の所得は 4 万 9,000 ドルほどだった．

同局によると，4,600 万人を超える人々が貧困生活を送っていた．1959 年の調査開始以来最多の数値である．そのうちの 4 分の 1 超が黒人とヒスパニックであり，12% がアジア人，10% が非ヒスパニック系白人だった．

変わらぬ景気対策もある．フルタイムで通年の仕事を持って働き続ける女性の収入は平均して同じ待遇の男性の 77% でしかない．

医療保険のない人々の人数は，前年度は 4,900 万人からほぼ 5,000 万人に増加した．しかしその比率は 16.3% で，2009 年度と同じ比率である．

医療保険を持つアメリカ人のほとんどは，保険を雇用者から取得している．経済政策協会のエリス・グールド氏によると，18 歳から 24 歳までの人々は少なくとも自分たちの雇用主の医療保険に加入している．しかし，国の新たな医療保険法によって，若者には障害がほとんどなくなった．

グールド氏「『医療保険制度改革』は，若い成人に対する職場での保険適用の下落を食い止める重要な役割を演じました．『患者保護医療費軽減法』は通常，医療保険制度改革として知られていますが，若い成人が 26 歳になるまで，両親の雇用主が保険提供者になった医療保険証の使用を許可する条項が含まれています」．

専門家は貧困の最大の原因は，失業であると言っている．およそ 1,400 万人のアメリカ人が失業している．何百万もの人々が職探しを止めて，もっと長く働けると願うことを諦めている．

ネバダ州のラスベガスはカジノやホテルで有名な都市である．だがラスベガスは不況の影響を色濃く受け，住宅市場の崩壊がそれに輪をかけた．元建設作業員のリチャード・スキャンロン氏は障害者であるが，健常者の友人らも失業しているという．

リチャード・スキャンロン「10〜15 年前はラスベガスで職が見つからなければどこに行っても見つからないと言われるほどでした．いまはラスベガスでも職はないのです」．

ファミリープロミスは政府系団体で，国民の求職や住宅取得を支援している．所長のテリー・リンデマン氏によると，ラスベガスのファミリープロミスは短期間住宅を提供してくれる宗教団体と連携して取り組んでいる．

【Reading Comprehension Questions 解答】
1. T 2. T 3. F 4. F 5. T 6. F 7. T 8. F 9. T 10. F

【Listening Comprehension Questions 解答】

This is IN THE NEWS in VOA Special English. A new report says the (poverty) (rate) in the United States last year was the (highest) since (1993). The official rate was (15.1) percent, up from 14.3 percent in 2009. Poverty meant yearly (income), or earnings, of less than (twenty-two) (thousand) (three) (hundred) dollars for a family of four.

【English Composition 解答】

1. The American recession lasted from December of 2007 to June of 2009.

2. About fourteen million Americans are unemployed.

3. Las Vegas, Nevada, is famous for its casinos and hotels.

Unit 9. アメリカの小学生，日本の被災者を支援

【訳例】

　何人かのアメリカの小学生が折り紙で鶴を折っている．児童は，3月11日に起きた東日本大震災と津波による犠牲者を偲んでいると表明したいのだ．

　40名近い日系アメリカ人児童がニュージャージー州のリッジウッドにあるサマービル小学校に通っている．総勢525名の小学生は東日本大震災の話を聞いた．だから，彼らは自分たちの学校を折り鶴で飾っている．児童たちは日本の人々のために早期復興を願っている．

　美術教師のサマンサ・スタンクウィッツは，小学生は，この折り鶴活動によって犠牲者への共感を表しているという．

　サマンサ・スタンクウィッツ「児童にとって折り鶴は象徴的であっても，自分たちが積極的に関わっていると感じることができる方法なのです」．

　児童は小学校の図書館で鶴を折りながら自分の考えを述べた．

　少年「折り鶴は希望のシンボルです．だから僕たちは日本の犠牲者の希望のためにたくさんの鶴を折っています」．

　少女「皆で他の国の人々に思いやりを持つことができ，とてもうれしいです」．

　少女「私は日本の人たちのことを考えると悲しくなります．とても悲しくなるのです．でも，私たちが皆で日本の人たちを助けたいと考えていることを感じると，とても嬉しくなります」．

　支援は折り鶴だけではない．小学校の校長であるローナ・オートサントス氏は，サマービル小学校の児童が災害救助機関に寄付するためにおよそ2,000ドルの寄付金を集めたと述べている．

　ローナ・オートサントス氏「私たちはこの寄付金をアメリカの赤十字とセーブ・ザ・チルドレンに寄付する予定です．この2つの機関は災害現場である日本で日本の人々を支援する用意が整っています」．

　小学校にはさまざまなタイトルの週間番組を制作する放送部がある．4年生の教師であるガブリエル・キング氏はこのクラブの顧問をしており，児童は小学校の活動に参加しているという．

ガブリエル・キング氏「震災が起きた時，児童たちは日本の人々のことを他の児童に分かってもらうために，自分たちには何ができるのかを知りたがっていました．ですから，私たちは震災についての思いを表明するために，折り紙で鶴を折ろう，折り鶴をしようと決めたのです」．

アメリカ人の児童の中には，他の形で日本の犠牲者に哀悼の意を表した者もいた．川村泰久氏はニューヨーク在住の日本総領事館の副総領事で，以下のように述べている．

川村泰久氏「一人の少女が2日前に総領事館に立ち寄り，自分で描いた絵を渡してくれました．その絵は日本とアメリカが太平洋を超えて握手をしている絵で『私たちはあなた達と一緒にいます』と書かれていました．私たちは大変感動し，少女の絵に心を動かされました」．

これこそ VOA スペシャル・イングリシュの教育レポートです．アメリカコーネル大学の東アジアプログラムでは，折り鶴の授業計画と指導案を提供しています．voaspecialenglish.com のウェブサイトでリンクしています．スティーブ・エンバーが担当しました．

【Reading Comprehension Questions 解答】
1. T 2. F 3. F 4. T 5. F 6. T 7. F 8. F 9. T 10. T

【Listening Comprehension Questions 解答】
This is the VOA Special English Education Report. (Cranes) are large birds with long legs and necks. In Japan and other East Asian cultures, they (represent) (luck) and (long) (life). Japanese (tradition) says a person who (folds) one (thousand) paper cranes (gets) the right to (make) a wish.

【English Composition 解答】
1. Some schoolchildren in the United States have been folding cranes.
2. We will be donating (will donate でも可) that money to the American Red Cross.
3. One American young girl dropped by the consulate a couple days ago.

Unit 10. 頭痛ですか．悩んでいるのは，あなただけではありません．

【訳例】

アメリカ頭痛財団によると 4,500 万人を超える人々が慢性頭痛に苦しんでいる．このような頭痛はひどい痛みがひいても，またぶり返すこともある．頭痛には治りづらいものもあり，治療に時間がかかるものもある．しかし現在多くの専門家が頭痛治療に取り組み，主に慢性頭痛の軽減に取り組んでいる．

アメリカ頭痛コンソーシアムは7つの組織が参加している団体である．この団体はいわゆる偏頭痛治療の改善に取り組んでいる．毎月2週間はこの種の頭痛に見舞われる人々がいる．頭痛財団によると偏頭痛に悩む人々の 70% が女性である．

頭部に圧迫感があり，ガンガンとした頭痛がする人もいる．他にはキリキリと鋭い刃物を頭に差し込まれたような痛みを伴う場合もある．アメリカでは偏頭痛で欠勤する日が毎年少なくとも1億5,000万日にも上っている．偏頭痛は軽い時もある．しかし，通常の生活が送れなくなるくらい深刻な痛みになる場合もある．

メリーランド州のエリコットシティに住むカーチス・クローリー氏は偏頭痛に悩む一人だ．彼は子供の頃も頭痛に悩まされた．どんな頭痛だったかは覚えていないという．しかし大人になってひどい頭痛に苦しんだ時に，医師らは彼の頭痛が偏頭痛であると診断した．

現在クローリー氏は映画やビデオを制作し，監督している．彼は頭痛が何か月もなく過ごすこともあるという．しかし，その後1か月に3度も偏頭痛に見舞われることになる．彼の主治医は，薬を服用する場合は，頭痛の初期段階で飲めと指示している．痛みをコントロールすることができるからである．指示通りに服用しないと，痛みはひどくなる．クローリー氏は時々，病院で複数の薬を併用しなければならなくなることもあった．

偏頭痛を予防または軽減するために，毎日薬を飲まなければならない人もいる．他にはすでに起きている痛みを抑えるために薬を服用する人もいる．偏頭痛に見舞われている人々を診察する医師は，しばしば偏頭痛の特効薬であるトリプタンで知られている薬物群から頭痛薬を注文することがある．

ほとんどの偏頭痛は少なくとも一部は既成の薬剤が効く．ほとんどの人々が既成の薬剤を副作用なく服用している．医師らは偏頭痛治療にカフェインを使うこともある．おもしろいことに，カフェインは偏頭痛の原因にもなる．

医療専門家は，ミネソタ州ロチェスターに所在するメイヨ・クリニックの取り組みを長期に渡り認めてきた．メイヨ・クリニックは複数の食べ物が偏頭痛を引き起こす「引き金」になると考えている．その中にはチーズやアルコール飲料が含まれている．塩やグルタミン酸ナトリウムのような食品添加物も偏頭痛を引き起こすと考えられている．

メイヨ・クリニックは，患者に，過去に偏頭痛を起こさせたと思われる強い香りは避けるようにと話している．たとえ良い香りであっても，香水のような製品でひどい頭痛に見舞われた人もいる．

クリニックの専門家は偏頭痛で悩む人々に有酸素運動が効果的であると言っている．有酸素運動は心拍数を上げる．有酸素運動にはウォーキング，水泳，自転車に乗ることも含まれる．しかし，いきなり激しい運動を行うと頭痛の原因になることがある．だから，エネルギーを必要とする活動を始める前に軽い運動を行うと良い．

【Reading Comprehension Questions 解答】
1. T 2. F 3. T 4. F 5. T 6. T 7. F 8. F 9. F 10. T

【Listening Comprehension Questions 解答】
From VOA Learning English, this is Science in the News. I'm Steve Ember. Today Barbara Klein and I

tell about (headaches), the (pain) that (strikes) almost everyone at some time. Have you (had) a headache recently? If your (answer) is yes, you are like many millions of people worldwide who (experience) pain in the head. The pain can be (temporary), mild and (cured) by a simple (painkiller) like aspirin. Or, it can be (severe).

【English Composition 解答】
1. The National Headache Foundation says more than 45 million people in the United States suffer chronic headaches.
2. Doctors sometimes use caffeine to treat migraine headaches.
3. But a sudden start to hard exercise can cause headaches.

Unit 11. 障害者，新たな機会を得る
【訳例】

　政府の報告によると，障害者の人々は他の仕事に比べ用務員やビルの掃除人の職業についている人が多い．身体または精神障害を持つ人々は健常者よりも就職の機会が少ない傾向がある．障害者で職に就いている者は低い報酬の職業に就いており，健常者の仕事仲間よりも収入が低い場合が多い．

　メグ・グリゴル氏はシンクカレッジという名称の組織で働いている．この団体は，精神障害者に対しても課程を設け，社会的機会や職業訓練を提供できるように単科大学や総合大学を支援している．精神障害者の学生の多くがダウン症候群の障害を負っている．グリゴル氏は，精神障害を負っている学生も，大学に行くことによって将来の仕事でより多くの収入を得ようと望む他の健常者と同様に高等教育から得るものが大きいと語る．

　「たとえ学位を取得するためではなく雇用機会を改善するためであっても，知的障害者が大学に通う経済的影響を実証しようとしているところです」．グリゴル氏によると，知的障害者である学生が大学に行かない理由で最も多いのは，教員や両親が，彼らにできるわけがないと考えているから，という理由である．

　「実際に見たら，可能であると信じられるでしょう．これまでのキャリアや子どもの頃，人から知的障害者は大学に行けないと聞いたので，話を切り出されても型にはまった反応しかできないのです」．

　精神障害を持つ若者の大学進学を奨励するキャンペーンがある．以下の学生はそのキャンペーンに参加している一部の学生である．「大学入学は大きな挑戦です．高校で学べない新たなことを学ぶのです」．

　「私が大学に行くのは，教育を受け，私がどんな人間であるかを知るために行くのです．私は自分の家族や友人を誇りたいと思います」．

　バージニアコモンウェルス大学（VCU）にはその機会がある．精神障害を負っている学生は大

学で30か月授業を受けると特別修了証が授与される．リズ・ゲッゼル氏はVCUで中等教育後指導の責任者である．

彼女によると，VCUは，自分がどんなに芸術性があるかを知らずに過ごしていた一人の学生を見いだした．「彼はそれまで芸術に触れることがありませんでした．彼は写真のような自画像を描きました．われわれは彼の芸術性をもっと見つけています．彼らが持つ驚くほどの才能の発掘は，始まったばかりです」．こうした才能は，よい仕事を獲得し，社会で積極的に活動していくための能力なのである．

議会は，ADAとして知られているアメリカ障害者法を20年前に可決した．障害者が仕事につき公共交通や公共施設をもっと容易に使用できるように定めた法律である．

【Reading Comprehension Questions 解答】
1．T　2．T　3．F　4．F　5．T　6．F　7．T　8．F　9．F　10．T

【Listening Comprehension Questions 解答】
From VOA Learning English, welcome to (This) Is (America) in Special English. I'm Kelly Jean Kelly. And I'm Jim Tedder. Today we (look) (at) what's (happening) (with) (employment), (education) and (entertainment) for people with (disabilities).

【English Composition 解答】
1. Meg Grigal works with an organization called Think College.
2. There is a campaign to encourage young people with mental disabilities to consider college.
3. VCU discovered one student who had no idea how artistic he was.

Unit 12. アメリカ最高裁判所，医療保険改革法を支持するも移民法の大半を無効とする
【訳例】
　2010年年初に議会は「患者保護並びに医療費負担適正化法」を可決し，オバマ大統領はこれに署名を行った．この法律は「オバマケア」と呼ばれるようになった．この法律はオバマ政権では最重要な優先事項である．この法律は医療費が増大し，多くの人がしばしば深刻な金銭問題を抱えるアメリカ人を救済するために起草された．

　オバマケアはいわゆる「個人強制保険」と呼ばれている．この強制はすべてのアメリカ国民に2014年までに医療保険加入を強制し，加入しない場合は金銭的なペナルティを課すというものである．

　この法律の支持者は医療制度は特権的ではなく正しいと信じている．しかし多くの人々がこの法律に反対している．実際は26州がこの法律を覆そうと訴訟を起こしている．反対者は，国民が望まず，必要としていない保険商品を購入することを議会が強制するのは違憲だと言っている．

しかし世論調査によると，オバマケアはいくつかの点でアメリカ人にとても人気がある．予防医療への支払いを保険会社に求めている点，医療費の支払額の上限を禁じている点である．

それに加えて人気が高いのは，健康問題をすでに抱えている人々の保険加入拒否を禁じている点である．これは通常，既存欠陥と呼ばれている．オバマケアは26歳までは両親の保険に加入することを許可している．

オバマケアに賛否両論の多くの人々は，最高裁が医療改革法案を5対4で支持したことに驚いた．決定は大統領にとって大きな勝利だった．中心となったのは保守派で個人の強制的保険加入に反対であると思われていた最高裁長官のジョン・ロバーツ長官だった．しかし，ロバーツ長官は強制的な保険加入を税と呼び，最高裁ではリベラル派に属していた．同長官は，憲法と最高裁の決定で，議会は課税する権限があると述べたのである．

オバマ大統領は，医療費を払えないアメリカ人にとって，この決定は勝利であると述べた．

オバマ大統領「現在この政策について，だれが勝ち，だれが負けるのかといった多くの議論が行われていることは知っています．ワシントンDCではこのような政策はそういった傾向があります．しかし，そういう議論はピントが全くずれています．いかなる政治であっても，今日の決定は，この法律と最高裁の支持によって生活が安定するすべてのアメリカ国民にとって勝利となるのです」．

この法律は部分的に今年11月に行われる大統領選の前に発効する．2012年の大統領選でオバマ氏の対立候補である共和党のミット・ロムニー氏はこの決定に失望している．

共和党が政権を握り，上院を支配し，ミット・ロムニー氏が11月の大統領選に当選した場合，この法律は次年度には無効となる可能性がある．

【Reading Comprehension Questions 解答】
1. T 2. F 3. T 4. T 5. F 6. F 7. T 8. T 9. F 10. F

【Listening Comprehension Questions 解答】
Welcome to THIS IS AMERICA in VOA Special English. I'm Christopher Cruise.

Today, we will (look) (at) the recent United States (Supreme) (Court) rulings that (upheld) President Obama's health care law and (cancelled) parts of Arizona's immigration law. We also (report) on a case that (dealt) (with) the (sentencing) of murderers under the age of eighteen.

【English Composition 解答】
1. The law came to be known as "Obamacare."

2. But many are opposed to the law.

3. If Mr. Romney wins this November's election, the law could be cancelled next year.

Unit 13. 19世紀のアメリカのクリスマス

【訳例】

　19世紀前半は，クリスマスは現在とはかなり違った休日だった．法定休日ではないクリスマスを祝う決まった方法はなかった．全国の地域社会はそれぞれ異なる方法でクリスマスを祝った．クリスマスはイエス・キリストの誕生を祝うクリスチャンの重要な宗教的な日であると見る者もいた．他には，パーティーを開き，音楽を聴き，飲み食いして祝う者もいた．共同体によってはクリスマスをまったく祝わなかった．

　しかし，19世紀前半，アメリカ人は，多文化で古くからあるクリスマスの伝統と当時のアメリカの影響力を結びつけて祝日を新たに考案した．これまで話題にしたアンドリュー・ジャクソン，マーティン・ヴァン・ビューレンなどの歴史上の人物がどうクリスマスを祝ったのかを振り返ることもできる．

　1819年，アメリカ人人気作家のワシントン・アービングは5つの短編小説を書いて『スケッチ・ブック』という一冊の本にまとめた．

　短編小説は，農場で働く労働者を自宅に招いてクリスマスを祝う裕福なイギリス人地主を描いている．地主ははるか昔に祝われたであろう伝統的なクリスマスを再現した．アービングはこういった昔の伝統を振り返り，それを賞賛した．彼は異なる社会水準の人々が陽気で平和な休日をともに祝うという考えを好んだ．アービングはこのような求心力のあるクリスマスの伝統が現代のアメリカでは不足しているのではないかという懸念を表明しているようにも見える．

　ペン・レスタッドは『アメリカのクリスマス：歴史』という本を書いた．この本は求心力のある国民の休日となるクリスマスを，ゆっくりとではあるが，アメリカ人がどのようにして19世紀前半に形作っていったかが描かれている．レスタッドは異なる文化と宗教を背景に持つそれぞれのアメリカ人にとってクリスマスがどのような意味を持つのかを著している．多くの移民は，クリスマスの伝統を母国から持ち込んだ．

　アメリカ人が休日をどのように祝うかにあたり，宗教は大きな役割を果たす．カルビン派のクリスチャンはクリスマスを祝うことを禁じている．アメリカ聖公会やモラビア派のクリスチャンは礼拝や季節の飾りつけをしてクリスマスを称える．

　19世紀半ばまでに，クリスチャンの宗派は互いのクリスマスの意味を巡る宗教的相違いについて気にしなくなり，特別な方法でクリスマスを祝い始めた．

　クリスマスは家庭で祝う家族にとって大切な時間となった．より多くのアメリカ人クリスチャンがクリスマスツリーや贈り物をするヨーロッパの伝統の模倣を始めた．クリスチャンはクリスマスツリーがイエス・キリストを象徴し，新たな始まりの兆しであると信じていた．ドイツ人の移民は家庭に置かれた常緑樹であるクリスマスツリーの枝に灯りをともし，お菓子やおもちゃを置く伝統を持ち込んだ．

　家庭にクリスマスツリーを置く伝統はすぐに多くのアメリカ人家庭に広まった．人々にプレゼントをする習慣も広まった．これらの伝統が流行るにつれて，現代の商業やビジネスがクリスマスと結びつき発展してきた．

クリスマスの人気が広がるにつれて，クリスマスを州の休日にすると宣言する州もあった．ルイジアナ州は1837年にクリスマスを公的な休日にした最初の州である．1860年までに他の14州がクリスマスを休日にした．1870年になってやっとユリシーズ・グラント大統領がクリスマスを国民の休日にしたのである．

【Reading Comprehension Questions 解答】
1. T　2. F　3. F　4. T　5. T　6. F　7. T　8. F　9. T　10. F

【Listening Comprehension Questions 解答】
From VOA Learning English, welcome to The Making of a (Nation), our (weekly) program of American (history) for people learning American English. I'm Steve Ember. Today Shirley Griffith and I (present) a special program on (Christmas) (traditions) in the United States during the (first) (half) of the (19th) (century).

【English Composition 解答】
1. In 1819, an American writer Washington Irving published a book.
2. Many immigrants brought Christmas traditions from their own countries.
3. Christmas became an important time for families to celebrate at home.

Unit 14. アメリカ人は食卓を囲み，給仕し，買い物をして感謝祭を祝うのか
【訳例】
　作家のオー・ヘンリーは，感謝祭は実にアメリカ的な一日であると言っている．感謝祭は宗教的な休日ではない．しかし，崇高な意味がある．アメリカ人の中には感謝祭の前日や感謝祭祝日の朝に礼拝に参加する者もいる．
　家族と長距離旅行を楽しむ者もいる．お祝いの中心である晩餐を楽しむのだ．多くのアメリカ人にとって，感謝祭は家族全員がそろう唯一の時である．感謝祭の祝日は家族が再会する日なのである．
　感謝祭は毎年11月第4木曜日に祝われる．アメリカでは11月は秋である．秋は農作物の収穫の時期である．アメリカに最初に来たヨーロッパの入植者は自分たちの農作物を収穫した時，収穫を祝い感謝を捧げた．彼らは豊作を神に感謝した．多くの人々が感謝祭祝日に感謝を捧げているが，農作物の豊作に対してだけではないだろう．
　サーシャ・バイショフはワシントン出身である．彼女は今年，息子のセバスチャンに感謝している．「だから私の感謝祭は感謝する日なのです．愛している者や物をしっかりと抱きしめる日なのです．今年はわが家に戻る私の愛するセバスチャンに感謝します．」
　伝承によると，イギリス出身のピルグリムの入植者たちは1621年に最初の感謝祭を祝った．

入植者がアメリカの各地で初期の感謝祭を祝った証拠が残っている．しかし，ピルグリムの感謝祭の話は最も人気がある．

　ピルグリムは宗教的な反体制派であり，イギリスの圧政から逃れてきた人々である．彼らは，最初はオランダに逃れた．そしてオランダを去り，北米に植民国家を設立した．ピルグリムは，後にマサチューセッツのプリマスと知られる場所に 1620 年に上陸した．

　彼らの大西洋横断は困難な航海だった．アメリカに上陸した最初の 1 か月も大変な日々だった．およそ 100 人のピルグリムが秋に上陸したが，間もなく冬となった．寒い月が続き，半数が死亡した．

　春が来ると，ピルグリムたちは農作物を植え始めた．名前がスカントというネイティブ・アメリカンのインディアンが彼らを支えた．夏が終わると，ピルグリムたちはトウモロコシとオオムギの大量の収穫時期を迎えた．冬を過ごすことができる十分な量の食料だった．

　ピルグリムたちは収穫を感謝する式典を開こうと決めた．その頃の資料によると，ピルグリムのリーダーであるウィリアム・ブラッドフォードが下半期に日を設定した．彼は近くのインディアン部族も招待した．

　感謝祭の式典は 3 日間続いた．多くの食料があった．アヒル，ガチョウ，シチメンチョウなどの野鳥も含む食事だった．アメリカの植民地が大きくなるにつれ，多くの町と入植地が感謝祭や収穫を祝う式典を催した．それから 240 年ほど経ってから，感謝祭はやっと国民の祝日となったのである．

【Reading Comprehension Questions 解答】
1. F　2. T　3. F　4. T　5. F　6. T　7. F　8. T　9. T　10. F

【Listening Comprehension Questions 解答】
Welcome to This Is America from VOA Learning English. I'm Steve Ember.
And I'm Kelly Jean Kelly. (Imagine) the smell of sliced apples and spices like cinnamon and ginger all (mixed) (together) and (baked). Then let everything (cool) (down) and add a little sugar on top. For many Americans, that smell — the smell of apple pie — is a favorite part of (Thanksgiving) Day. Today we (report) on the history of the holiday and how Americans (are) (celebrating) this year.

【English Composition 解答】
1. The writer O. Henry called Thanksgiving the one day that is purely American.
2. Thanksgiving is celebrated every year on the fourth Thursday of November.
3. When spring came, the Pilgrims began to plant crops.

Unit 15. 新研究：外国人留学生はアメリカを改善しスピーディにする
【訳例】
　多くの若い女性は15歳の誕生日（スペイン語）にお祝いします．しかし，まず，アメリカの外国人留学生について話をします．最近の報告では，アメリカ政府は，外国人がアメリカに滞在するために，高等教育の学位取得に容易に取り組めるよう便宜をはかるべきであると論じています．VOAのジョー・デカプアからの報告をマリオ・リッターがお知らせします．

　アメリカは，特に科学，工学分野で多くの外国人留学生を教育している．しかし外国人留学生は教育を終えた後，アメリカのために何をしてくれるのだろうか．
　3名の経済学者は調査を行うことにした．調査チームの代表者はボルダーにあるコロラド大学のキース・マスカス教授である．同教授によると，2001年の9.11テロ事件以降，アメリカの大学院課程に入学するのが難しくなった地域もある．
　当時，多くのアメリカ官庁職員や教育者らは外国人留学生を制限すると科学の発達や革新が損なわれると警告した．「私は，そうですね，大変興味深いと考えますが，それは本当に正しいと言えるのでしょうか」．
　マスカス教授はイェール大学のアームド・マスフィク・ムバラク教授とアイダホ大学のエリック・スタン教授と調査を行った．3人は多くのデータを収集した．教授らは1970年代から1990年代後半までアメリカのトップレベルの科学工学大学で研究した7万5,000人の博士後期課程の学生を調査した．
　教授らは多様性が生産性と効率性を改善することを解明した．言い換えると，アメリカのアメリカ人と外国人留学生が混在すると，大学や職場が改善されスピーディになるのである．
　「ネットワークと研究室の科学には関連性があるようです．大学院生とポスドクの学生，すべての人が科学のある要素をどう専門化するかの問題についてうまく機能するようになるのです．それは学部での教育と大学院での教育が数学または研究室の科学など何であれ，問題を考えるための異なるアプローチを与えることができるのです」．
　「そしてこれらの人々は一緒に集うことができ，結果的にさらにダイナミックな思考過程を生み出せるよう互いに相手の考えを引き出すことができるのです．そのような多様性によってさらに良いアイデアを得ることができます」．
　マスカス教授は，教授のグループが行った調査結果によると，アメリカは外国人留学生に対する政策を変更するべきであると述べている．現在，留学生は，たとえ大学が奨学金を提供する場合でも，本人または家族が教育費を支払うことができると証明する必要がある．
　マスカス教授は，外国人留学生がグリーンカードを取得しやすくなるような政策を政府が行うべきであると指摘している．そうすれば留学生はアメリカに永住することができる．同教授によると，カナダやオーストラリアなどは，科学技術または工学のPhD取得を目指す留学生は永住者となっている．しかし，アメリカでは，アメリカに残りたい留学生は，自分たちに一時的なビザを発行する地元の雇用主を探す必要がある．

【Reading Comprehension Questions 解答】

1. T 2. F 3. F 4. F 5. T 6. T 7. F 8. T 9. T 10. F

【Listening Comprehension Questions 解答】

Welcome back to As It Is. Today we will (be) (talking) (about) people who (move) (to) the United States from other countries. Some are immigrants who (bring) their traditions with them. On our show, we (look) (at) families from (Latin) (American) nations.

【English Composition 解答】

1. We talk about foreign students in the United States.

2. They found that diversity improved productivity and efficiency.

3. The U.S. should change its policies toward foreign students.

付録　役に立つサイト

オンライン辞書
  http://ejje.weblio.jp/（Weblio 英和和英辞典）
  http://www.alc.co.jp/（アルク英辞郎 on the Web）
  http://www.merriam-webster.com/（Merriam-Webster）

検索（日本語）
  https://www.google.co.jp

コンコーダンス（文字列で検索するサイト：英語）
  http://www.webcorp.org.uk/

みんなの知識　ちょっと便利帳（日本語）
  http://www.benricho.org/

アメリカのことがわかるホームページ

アメリカ早分かり（アメリカ大使館が提供するアメリカに関する公式情報）
  http://aboutusa.japan.usembassy.gov/

アメリカ大使館の日本語訳がある PDF 書籍
  http://aboutusa.japan.usembassy.gov/j/jusaj-translations.html

アメリカの地図と主要都市間距離
  http://www.usatourist.com/japanese/tips/maps.html#map

アメリカ大統領選結果
  http://www.uselectionatlas.org/RESULTS/

アメリカ大統領選アトラス
  http://uselectionatlas.org/

アメリカ電子図書館
  http://elibraryusa.state.gov/

日米関係資料・ジャーナルのホームページ

外交安全保障政策に関する史料（堂場文書）
  http://kw.maruzen.co.jp/ln/mc/mc_doc/doba.pdf

同志社大学アメリカ研究所
  http://www.america-kenkyusho.doshisha.ac.jp/overview/overview.html

American Diplomacy
 http://www.unc.edu/depts/diplomat/
ハーバード大学ジャーナル（Harvard Asia Pacific Review）
 http://www.hcs.harvard.edu/~hapr/index.html
大阪大学大学院杉田研究室（アメリカ研究ゼミ）
 http://sugita.us/

> アメリカ在外機関

US Embassy（アメリカ大使館）
 http://japanese.japan.usembassy.gov/index.html
USPACOM（米太平洋軍司令部）
 http://www.pacom.mil/
USFJ（在日米軍）
 http://www.usfj.mil/

参 考 文 献

- A. ハミルトン，J. ジェイ，J. マディソン『ザ・フェデラリスト』斎藤真，中野勝郎翻訳（岩波書店，1999 年）
- 有賀貞『アメリカ史2』（山川出版社，1993 年）
- 団藤重光『法学の基礎』第2版（有斐閣，2007 年）
- 外務省「東日本大震災に係る米軍による支援（トモダチ作戦）」『外務省』（2011 年）（http://www.mofa.go.jp/mofaj/saigai/pdfs/operation_tomodachi.pdf）
- 本間千枝子，有賀夏紀，石毛直道『世界の食文化：アメリカ』XII.（農山漁村文化協会，2004 年）
- 厚生労働省「医療上の必要性の高い未承認薬・適応外薬検討会議公知申請への該当性に係る報告書：プロプラノロール塩酸塩，偏頭痛における頭痛発作の予防」『厚生労働省』（2013 年）（http://www.mhlw.go.jp/seisakunitsuite/bunya/kenkou_iryou/iyakuhin/kaihatsuyousei/dl/s0831-01.pdf）
- Library Of Congress "America's Stroy: Christmas Day December 25" *Library Of Congress* （http://www.americaslibrary.gov/jb/modern/jb_modern_xmas_1.html）
- NEDO「産業技術，ライフサイエンス：偏頭痛の開始を察知して，痛みを取り除く装置（米国）」『NEDO 海外レポート』御原幸子翻訳，No.958，（NEDO，2005 年）http://www.nedo.go.jp/content/100106343.pdf）
- The University of Chicago Library "Turkeys Gobble Gobble" *The University of Chicago Library* （http://guides.lib.uchicago.edu/content.php?pid=277886&sid=2289533）

■著者紹介

佐藤　晶子　（さとう　あきこ）

現　　　職：近畿大学経営学部非常勤講師（英語）
　　　　　　阪南大学学習支援室学習アドバイザー（英語）
最終学歴：大阪大学大学院言語文化研究科博士後期課程
学　　位：修士（言語文化学）

主著
（共著）一般社団法人日本翻訳連盟（JTF）編著『JTFほんやく検定公式問題集』（アルク，2011年）
（共訳）田中利幸，ティム・マコーミック，ゲリー・シンプソン編著『再論　東京裁判：何を裁き，何を裁かなかったか』（大月書店，2012年）
（共訳）杉田米行編『アメリカ社会への多面的アプローチ』（大学教育出版，2005年）

語学シリーズ第3巻
ボイス・オブ・アメリカ（VOA）ニュースで学ぶ英語　レベル1

2014年11月10日　初版第1刷発行
2017年4月30日　初版第2刷発行

■著　　者――佐藤晶子
■発 行 者――佐藤　守
■発 行 所――株式会社　大学教育出版
　　　　　　〒700-0953　岡山市南区西市855-4
　　　　　　電話（086）244-1268　FAX（086）246-0294
■印刷製本――モリモト印刷㈱

Ⓒ Akiko Sato 2014, Printed in Japan
検印省略　落丁・乱丁本はお取り替えいたします。
本書のコピー・スキャン・デジタル化等の無断複製は著作権法上での例外を除き禁じられています。本書を代行業者等の第三者に依頼してスキャンやデジタル化することは，たとえ個人や家庭内での利用でも著作権法違反です。
ISBN978-4-86429-272-6